Back in the USSR

Back in the USSR
Heroic Adventures in Transnistria

Rory MacLean

photographs by Nick Danziger

unbound

This edition first published in
2014

Unbound
4–7 Manchester Street
Marylebone
London W1U 2AE
www.unbound.co.uk

Patriotic Soviet captions approved
by the Central Committee of the
Communist Party of the Soviet
Union for the 60th Anniversary
of the Great October Socialist
Revolution.

Designed by Mark Thomson
Assisted by Rob Payne
Image processing by David Mallows

A CIP record for this book is
available from the British Library

ISBN (limited edn):
978–1–78352–061–9

ISBN (trade edn):
978–1–78352–062–6

ISBN (ebook):
978–1–78352–063–3

Printed in Riga, Latvia by
Livonia Print

frontispiece: 'Peoples of the world!
Proletarians of all nations! Unite!'

1 **Journey of a Faithful Traveller** 1

2 **Motherland** 11

3 **Heroes and Traitors** 19

4 **Big Brother** 31

5 **Che Guevara High School of Political Leadership** 41

6 **In Praise of Propaganda** 49

7 **'To the bottom, Comrade!'** 57

8 **Cultural Dreamer** 67

9 **Earthly Paradise** 75

10 **True to his Word** 83

11 **Factory** 95

12 **I Believe in Miracles** 105

13 **Freedom from Fear** 113

14 **Our Glorious Future** 121

15 **Swan Song** 131

Transnistrian timeline 144
Acknowledgments 145
Subscribers 146

↖ Harrods
(1685 miles)

• Kamenka

Ribnita •   • Cobasna
              Ammunition
              Dump

MOLDOVA

TRANSNISTRIA

Dubasari •

Tashlyk •

Chisinau ⊛

Bendery •   ⊙ Tiraspol
              •
             Chitcani

ROMANIA

Kurchurgan •
Power Plant

Dniester

Dniester

Dniester

Monaco
↙ (2315 miles)

Moscow ↗
(800 miles)

UKRAINE

Odessa

BLACK SEA

CRIMEA

1

Journey of a Faithful Traveller

Sunlight sparkles off the broad Dniester River. Grapes glisten in verdant vine terraces above Kamenka. Smugglers' tracks wind across the snow and into silent woods. Patriotic oligarchs in Gucci tracksuits hunt wild boar with AK-47s. A springtime breeze loosens the blossoms from the apricot trees, scattering them over Russian peacekeepers guarding old Soviet munitions dumps. At the Che Guevara High School of Political Leadership the party faithful learn how to launch 'spontaneous actions' while sustaining the half lotus yoga position. Across Tiraspol a young woman celebrates her escape from prostitution, then pays the price for freedom by recruiting other local girls to be trafficked to brothels abroad.

Comrades! Have you ever wondered what became of the socialist dream? What happened to the society of equals? Where all those Red Army generals, KGB colonels and go-getting Moscow tycoons went when they retired? It – and they – live on in Transnistria.

Sort of.

Transnistria is a breakaway republic of a breakaway republic of the old Soviet Union: youthful yet venerable, ambitious but dreamy,

'Long live the Great October Socialist Revolution –
the start of humanity's historical journey away from
capitalism and to socialism!'

dirt poor and damn profitable. No bigger in size than Devon or Rhode Island, this sliver-thin nowhereland lies both on the eastern bank of the Dniester, one of the oldest geopolitical fault lines in Europe, and at the threshold of an heroic new age. It is proud, independent-ish and recognised by no other country in the world. It's also the home of my exclusive and elusive host.

Once he was known as New Soviet Man. He was heralded as an archetype, a master of his emotions, a 'higher social biologic being'. He could have been born in Moscow, Kiev or Vladivostok. His name might have been Vladimir, Arkady or Yakov. His singularity was unimportant for he'd risen above the cult of individuality to be a selfless everyman dedicated to spreading the socialist revolution.

But times change and – after the fall of the Berlin Wall – my host and his kind had to learn to think outside the box. He, as a *new* New Soviet Man, needed to keep his eyes on the deal. He began to study profit margins instead of the Great Path of the Party. He looked after Number One. He bought a lavish pied-à-terre in London and donned a Chanel balaclava to fight for Crimean 'independence'. He set up shell companies in Transnistria.

· Today most westerners – at least those of the younger generation – have lost the dream of the possibility of creating a better world. Many imagine no change in their lives greater than updating their iPad apps. They construct a solitary existence in a void of political apathy wishing for nothing more than faster wifi. Idealism looks pretty dead west of the Dniester.

But on its eastern shore New Soviet Man embraces bolder dreams (which always include at least one gold Cartier wristwatch). He and his super-elite peers buy industries not apps. Their Facebook friends own airlines and oil fields. Their tweets are followed in the Kremlin. Money enables them to glide all but unseen through life, except when promenading along the Croisette in Cannes. Naive cynics assert it's inconvenient for them that the great Union of Soviet

4

previous pages: In Transnistria old Soviet symbols and slogans are retained more than 20 years after the collapse of the USSR. At the Dniester Sanatorium in Kamenka, a hand-painted mural celebrates the physical and political health of body, mind and nation.

Socialist Republics was dumped in the trash can of history, but name another dying empire which has given its movers and shakers more golden opportunities?

They – the archetypes who got real – are united by the experience of Communism. Their quixotic and inequitable ideology lives on in the tender hearts of its proletariat (at least of those who haven't yet emigrated; the population of Transnistria has halved over the last 20 years). On the factory floors and across the fallow fields of its collective farms, dreamers and despots alike celebrate Transnistria's uniqueness as the only country in the world not to have recognised the collapse of the Soviet Union.

Dear readers, I invite you to join me and New Soviet Man on a journey into his republic's heart, as well as its numbered Swiss bank accounts. Together we will listen to Slavonic Dixieland music, plunge into the Dniester's frozen New Year waters, wait in awe with the head of national television for a telephone call from the great Vladimir Putin. We will meet the teenagers who dream of being sold to Chelsea or Spartak Moscow and the personable, attractive young women who – in a clever coup of political marketing – are 'sexing up' government ministries both online and in the flesh. We will come to understand what happens to a spunky factory manager after he wins four elections in a row and buys a couple too many S-Class Mercedes. We will see that same old leader crushed as Transnistria embraces the possibility – or at least the impression – of change. Finally we will realise that Communism no longer means Communism as such, but rather a 'special' relationship with Russia.

My friends, this volume is both a personal journey and an earnest exhortation. Believe me, it is time to dispel the myths about New Soviet Man's people's republic. The hour has come to bury the tired clichés that it is a black hole, a penniless smugglers' haven, a criminalised *terra incognita* kept in a state of suspended animation specifically to facilitate illegal activities. Transnistria is not the North

overleaf: On the 17th floor of a residential apartment building in the capital Tiraspol is the headquarters of the First Republican Television Channel. In its control room, a technician volunteers, 'Putin is a hero for us. He makes us proud again.' The sign above the desk reads, 'Do Not Litter'.

Korea of Europe. It is rather a land open for business, where the balalaikas ring out as the Great Game is played on, and the faithful traveller can find himself – with a little imagination plus a load of cash – back in the USSR.

Sort of.

Vladimir Putin has said his country reserves the right to stand up for ethnic Russians living outside its borders. Most Transnistrians wait for the president to act, even though 500 miles of Ukrainian territory separates their isolated mini-state and Russia.

2

Motherland

Communism is his pride and future. It is the glue of the people. The hammer and sickle rise like the sun in the republic's crest. The red star crowns the bold Transnistrian flag. Long live the proletarian zeal for revolution!

According to the scientific analysis of history, Communism rips power out of the hands of the capitalist class. Workers and their allies then wrestle the economy under social control. Labour becomes both a civic duty and a source of personal fulfilment. People realise their potential and – as oppressive class divisions are abolished – the state apparatus itself withers away in an ecstasy of equality. And so on. And so on.

New Soviet Man's driver dropped us off in the Bentley. At the end of an alley behind Tiraspol No. 3 Compulsory School stood the headquarters of the Communist Party of Transnistria. A concrete Lenin surveyed the front hall of the two-up two-down conversion. 'Iron Felix' Dzerzhinsky, first chairman of the Cheka and KGB, glowered from his portrait behind the Lavazza coffee machine.

'The Soviet Union is the place where I was born. It is my Motherland,' declared Oleg Khorzhan, striking his chest with his fist. His silver watch sparkled as he folded together his podgy fingers.

11

'Let live for centuries the name and work of Vladimir Ilyich Lenin! Fervently love the Soviet Motherland, persistently acquire knowledge and labour skills! Prepare yourselves to become active fighters for the task of Lenin, for Communism!'

'My job as Party leader is to preserve – and to carry forward – the positive attributes of the USSR: its power, its social guarantees, its absence of borders and, above all, its belief in tomorrow.'

'*Urrah!*' cheered New Soviet Man with feeling, because he'd noted that the watch was a Patek Philippe.

Since time immemorial (that is, about 200 years) Transnistria has been part of Greater Russia. But during the Second World War, Stalin reached west across the Dniester to seize neighbouring Romanian Moldova. He tacked it on to Slav Transnistria, creating the Moldavian Soviet Socialist Republic and – with it – not a few problems.

After the war hundreds of victorious Red Army officers retired to the unified republic. They built their dachas along its riverbanks, savouring the balmy southern climate and dreaming of further glories. Their opportunity came with the fall of the Berlin Wall.

In the early 1990s the Republic's expropriated, western, Moldovan half turned its back on the Slavic world. It declared Romanian to be its official language and joined both NATO's Partnership for Peace and the Council of Europe. In response an ambitious, Russian-born factory manager on the Dniester's eastern bank galvanised the nostalgic soldiers and eager oligarchs to retain their links with Moscow.

'On November 2nd, 1990 – in the upheaval following the fall of the Wall – I saw ordinary civilians shot on the Dubăsari Bridge,' Khorzhan told us with feeling, naming the river crossing where three Transnistrians were killed by Moldovan troops, thereby inflaming the 'war of independence'. 'I was 14 years old at the time. I saw how nationalistic feeling was being cultivated in Moldova, and how Moldovans turned against their brothers, even shooting them in the back. I realised then that I could not live in such a place. As soon as I finished high school I became a Communist.'

He signed up in Tiraspol, capital of the breakaway enclave, hoping that Party membership would wipe away the sudden sense of rootlessness. In those tumultuous days he didn't dwell on Communism's fragility or the dichotomy between its reality and its creators' visions. Like millions of others in fractured eastern Europe, he simply felt lost.

'I believed – and still believe – that all the former Soviet republics will one day join together again, not as a single state but as an economic union. This is not a dream; it's a reality for me.'

Behind Khorzhan hung a wall map of the old USSR, its 15 republics united in fraternal brotherhood. With the Union's dissolution, all the republics had become independent. Some – like Georgia and Moldova – had disintegrated into even smaller entities.

'People with such strong historical and economic connections are meant to live together for eternity,' he assured us, but then pointed an accusative finger at neighbouring Ukraine. 'I have been anxiously following the nonsense that the fascists in Ukraine have been performing. I welcome President Putin's desire to unite Russian soil.'

'As a westerner you will not understand the importance of the land, of the *soul* to us,' New Soviet Man explained to me, adjusting the handkerchief in his Dolce & Gabbana jacket. His personal style signifier was a pochette square bought from vintage stores. He had over 500 of them, choosing a different one every day depending on his mood and wardrobe. 'The western soul is like a fenced garden: well-nurtured, well-maintained, with a sensible structure. Our soul, our Slav *duscha*, is totally different. It is wild. It is open. It has no limit. It is like a vast steppe from which we get all that nourishes us, but in which we can become lost.'

Khorzhan reached across the desk to take New Soviet Man's hand in his own. The two men looked into each other's eyes with remarkable warmth, as if they were brothers reunited after many years. Khorzhan then rose from his melamine desk. He opened a cupboard to show off a red Communist rain shell, thousands of which had been handed out to supporters, and friends of supporters,

and friends of friends of supporters who couldn't resist freebies. He presented us each with a Party pen, noting with pride, 'It's made in Germany.

'Around the world young people wear the hammer and sickle on their T-shirts. Communist symbols are graffitied on walls. This is not nostalgia. Youngsters realise what is good for the planet. They understand that selfishness guarantees them no future,' he told us, emotion rising in his voice as he morphed Marxist–Leninism with anti-globalisation Newspeak. 'The Soviet leaders understood the importance of selflessness,' he shouted. 'Did Stalin lead an independent Georgia or the united Soviet Union? Was Nikita Khrushchev a Ukrainian politician or a great Soviet leader?'

As I wrestled with the subtleties of his argument, he puckered his lips and calmed himself. For a moment I wondered if he had lost his way in my host's limitless steppe. Khorzhan blinked away a nervous tick and explained in measured tones how after Transnistria's war of independence – which had claimed to be preserving Communism – the Communists were elbowed out of power.

'They stole our property,' he grumbled, a frown troubling his boyish looks. 'My comrades and I were arrested for organising a meeting and sentenced to one and a half years in prison. But Communist parties from around the world – even from Great Britain – sent telegrams of support and the sentence was commuted.'

The Party's office used to occupy the biggest single building in the country. Every state employee had been a member. Marxism–Leninism was the most powerful ideological weapon in the struggle against imperialism. But now his HQ had been relocated at the end of an alley.

'It wasn't fair,' sighed Khorzhan who isn't yet 40. His peevishness brought to mind the words of French Premier Georges Clemenceau who once wrote, 'Not to be a socialist at 20 is proof of want of heart; to be one at 30 is proof of want of head.'

16

previous pages: Lenin keeps an eye on a party worker in the office of Transnistria's last Communist Deputy. The fall of the Soviet Union was 'the greatest geopolitical disaster of the 20th century', said Vladimir Putin. His vision is to recreate Russian power, not to resurrect the failed USSR.

Yet since his release from prison (he was locked up for only 36 hours) Khorzhan and the authorities had found a way to work together, judging from his weight gain since his election to the Supreme Soviet.

'We modern Communists have left behind the old stereotypes,' he said with a wink to my smiling companion. 'We have accepted the market economy, the ownership of private property. For me it's no longer a question of everyone being equal but rather of fairness. I think that almost everyone on the planet recognises that there are only two possible courses: the dead end of selfishness or the road to fairness.'

We paused to savour his statement. In Transnistria Marx's visionary manifesto has been adjusted for the modern, mercantile age, the central principle of equality replaced with this notion of 'fairness'. New Soviet Man felt pleased to have tipped the peasant who polished his SUV that morning.

'Not everything that former Transnistrian president Igor Smirnov did was wise,' said Khorzhan, choosing his words with care, looking over his shoulder out of habit. Smirnov had been the spunky factory manager who'd led the 1990 insurgency, grabbed power and ordered Khorzhan's arrest. 'But at least he never turned against our monuments. He kept our historical symbols alive: Lenin still stands in most town squares; Tiraspol's main street is named after the October Revolution. These symbols enable us to respect history, and to avoid repeating errors, and so will help our Motherland to find its way toward the future.'

With those stirring words the last Communist deputy in the last Supreme Soviet smiled sweetly, offered us his plump hand, then opened the door to usher us back into the real world.

As soon as we were out of earshot my New Soviet Man dropped his smile and scoffed, 'He is dust.' Meaning history, food for worms, dead.

3

Heroes and Traitors

Snow flurries danced in the air, caught the slipstream of a shivering
trolley bus, whipped into the faces of the flat-capped men towing
wooden carts toward the market. At a bus stop thick-set commuters
waited in battle fatigues. Young women, their faces haloed in deep,
fur-lined hoods, stamped the winter cold out of their high-heeled
boots. The ancient trolley shuddered to a halt, its contacts sparking
and crackling on the iced overhead wires. The driver swung down
from his cab, hoisted himself up onto the roof and – with raw
hands blackened with grease – hacked the ice off the contacts with
a broken bayonet. He eased the arms back onto the lines, ignored
the passengers and continued on his way, past *babushkas* selling
tangerines frozen as hard as orange rocks and twin billboards
celebrating the new president's surprise victory. On the first poster
Yevgeny Shevchuk, the 'outsider' who had won the recent general
election and ended factory manager Smirnov's 20-year reign,
declared, 'We need change!' In the second poster he looked in the
opposite direction and promised, 'There will be order!'

Beyond the billboards a graphite Porsche with tinted windscreen

'Vodka is best drunk in threes,' volunteered
Vladimir Nikoluk, among the most honest –
and least fearful – men in the pariah state.
'If you drink alone, you are an alcoholic. If two
people drink, a man and a woman, it's romance.
But with three drinkers, you have the perfect
number of companions.'

jumped the traffic light. Two Militiamen – there are no police in Transnistria – looked the other way.

On that bright, winter morning Vladimir Nikoluk wasn't working. It was his 58th birthday and he and his pretty, petite, third wife Alexandra were in the mood for celebration.

'We talk, we cook, we drink, and we try to hear each other above the racket,' he roared to us in welcome, pouring glasses of Ukrainian *Khlebnaya Sleza*. On the tongue the cool, clean vodka tasted of freshly-baked white bread. 'The first and last glass must be swallowed in a single gulp. The ones in between are up to you,' he advised. 'But understand that your glass will never be empty in my house.'

Nikoluk was a big, generous man with a salt-and-pepper goatee beard, fist-flattened nose and immense hands. He introduced himself as a 'maximalist': buying the best food, cooking the largest quantities, snatching the most beautiful women in the country and – when necessary – marrying them. 'No one calls me a minimalist,' he warned in a voice loud enough to shake snow off the roof. He was an engineer, head of the Union of Builders, and the least cautious man in Transnistria.

In an icy parking lot, he loaded an oil drum barbecue with charcoal and set it alight with a blow torch.

'We will eat *kostitza*,' he declared, flourishing two platters of home-cured pork cut as thick as his thumbs. When he threw them on the grill one could almost hear the pig squeal. 'No T-bone steak ever tasted as good.'

Nikoluk was born near the source of the Dniester in the western Ukraine. The region had been part of Poland before the Second World War, then part of the Soviet Union, then an independent state. Despite the changes, its people had retained characteristic Polish ambition and industriousness. At technical college in L'viv, Nikoluk and his classmates were taught that they would become the best engineers in the USSR.

22

previous pages: Like 97.2% of Transnistrians, he believes that the breakaway republic should be recognised as an independent nation linked to Russia, and not a part of Moldova.

'"You are the leaders, the Jews of the Jews," they told us. "Nothing can stand in your way." That wasn't the usual Communist approach,' he assured us, rubbing a little more lustre off the old Soviet archetypes.

On graduation Nikoluk was posted down river in Soviet Moldova. The young crane mechanic liked the republic with its southern women and heady local wine. At the first Builders' Day festival he drank too much of it and told the factory boss that he'd take his job within two years. And he did.

'Success was the religion of the L'viv Technological Institute,' he said, lighting a Cuban cigar. As its smoke mingled with the aroma of scorched meat he added, 'I buy them on the Uruguayan market. They are cheaper that way.'

In 1990 Nikoluk breathed similar ambition into the 'war of independence', becoming vice-director of the 'Strike Committee for an Independent Transnistria'.

'In Moldova people chanted "Moldova for ethnic Moldovans" and called me an incomer,' he recalled, refilling our glasses, lobbing the first empty bottle into the snow. 'Where could I go? I joined the comrades who wanted to maintain links with Russia. I rang Gorbachev and met Deputy Premier Ryzhkov. I told them, "The Soviet Union is falling apart." They assured me that it would never happen. But it did.'

He sucked on his cigar.

'For the next half a year I wore a flak jacket. I carried a gun. I had my special "missions". I fought to preserve our Motherland.'

We raised our glasses to Motherlands which brought tears to Nikoluk's hooded blue eyes. New Soviet Man moved next to him, placing a hand on his shoulder, speaking so quickly and passionately that I could not follow the conversation.

As they bonded (or perhaps struck some deal), Nikoluk's wife Alexandra emerged from their ground-floor apartment, tottering on her heels between the snowdrifts, bearing plates of pickled watermelon and *salo*, salt-cured slabs of fatback pork, as well as a steaming jug of *ukha* fish broth – concocted from freshwater perch and vodka – and reputed to prevent hangovers. Behind her the patched, five-storey block was bisected by gas and drain pipes, its balconies boxed in and curtained against the cold. At an upper window a housewife had broken off from her morning chores. She leaned out of her window to smoke a cigarette, tapping the ash onto the frozen garden below.

'Vodka is best drunk in threes,' cheered Nikoluk, turning back to me as he cracked open another bottle. 'If you drink alone, you are an alcoholic. If two people drink, a man and a woman for example, they are interested in something else. But with three drinkers, you have the perfect number of companions.' He refilled our glasses and he added, 'Try the blood sausage.'

With independence Nikoluk – now a large fish in a very small pond – had grasped the chance to rebuild Transnistria's damaged infrastructure. He won the contracts to repair the Dniester bridges. He went on to supply the steel for all of the republic's petrol stations.

'I benefited from the situation,' he confessed, crunching the tension out of his neck. 'Also Transnistria – lying between Western Europe and Ukraine – has 360 kilometres of open border. What else do I need to say? All the big money has come because of our unrecognised status, through contraband of one sort or other like in the US during Prohibition. But I did no smuggling. I tolerated no corruption. I paid taxes, unlike Big Brother.'

'Tell me about Big Brother,' I asked.

'As you know, Big Brother has a buy-and-sell ideology. They are interested only in profit. They make money. I make things.'

He laid down his cigar, scraped the charcoal off the steaks then sprayed them with spirit. Flames leapt into the air, melting snow around the barbecue's base.

'In the Soviet years people had stability, social guarantees, their own apartment,' he reminisced, changing the subject. 'I still have those things, plus a new Lexus, only now I must work 36 hours every day.'

In time more glasses were raised and emptied and the steaks were done. We wove our way indoors – heads buzzing, fighting for focus – and Nikoluk twisted his broad shoulders through the doorways between bedroom suites and fitness room, showing off the newly fitted kitchen and sauna converted from an old bomb shelter. On a huge widescreen TV in the living room his four-year-old daughter Maria watched Ukrainian cartoons at top volume.

'Sony Bravia,' said New Soviet Man with a nod of approval.

In his swanky home and our alcoholic haze we fancied for a moment that Pure Communism had been achieved in our lifetime. We also joked about pigs learning to fly. I asked Nikoluk how he had found the apartment on central Karl Marx Street.

'I was just lucky,' he laughed, his expansive spirit filling the room with crackling energy. Behind him the ice maker clinked in a stainless steel American fridge-freezer.

His table groaned under the weight of yet more food: platters of charcuterie, plates of marinated tomatoes, three varieties of potato, half a dozen cheeses as well as the butter-tender *kostitza* pork. In eastern Europe it is said that guests are welcomed with everything on the table, while in the West the best food is kept in the cupboard. There were also more bottles. Every time a new vodka was opened and the glasses filled, little Maria tried to recap it.

We ate, drank, danced then debated historical materialism and business synergy. Maria lay on a toy tiger rug and turned up the television again. Around nightfall Nikoluk barked at her, an edge of unpredictability flashing in his eyes. Alexandra noticed it and slipped out of her chair to nestle in his lap like a small and delicate bird. He was twice her size, and twice her age.

'I found her working at the Dom Soviet,' he said as if discussing the netting of a rare specimen for a collection. 'Every time I passed the city hall I'd call by her office and say, "Your uncle is back to see you again."'

'I didn't notice him at first,' chirped Alexandra, smiling to reveal her new dental braces. 'But he was very persistent, and very sly.'

Nikoluk bellowed with delight, wrapping her in his beefy arms. The short sleeves of his black T-shirt emphasised his biceps. Her proximity mellowed him and in a surprisingly wistful voice he said to me, 'It was always my dream to travel. But I can't, even with my two passports.'

All Transnistrians have a Transnistrian passport, which is useless for foreign travel. Hence most also possess a Russian, Ukrainian or Moldovan document, but even those aren't valid for Europe without a visa. No wonder cars with Transnistrian licence plates are known as 'trolley buses', unable to escape their closed circuit, forbidden from venturing further west than Moldova or further east than Moscow.

Nikoluk's inability to travel wasn't his only regret.

'Our country Transnistria was the basis of the old Moldavian Soviet Socialist Republic. So why are we now just a forgotten island between Moldova and Ukraine? No one is happy with the present status, yet for 20 years nothing has changed. If Europe really wants to end our isolation, they should simply welcome Transnistria into the EU.'

'Moscow will never let Transnistria stray out of reach,' pointed out New Soviet Man. 'In any case, its ill-defined status is good for business.' Our thoughts were on events unfolding over the border in Ukraine. Crimea had been annexed by Moscow, strengthening its 'indivisible bond' with the Russian Federation, while heavily armed pro-Russian rebels were wreaking bloody havoc on the ground and in the skies above eastern Ukraine.

New Soviet Man seemed delighted with the business

opportunities soon to arise in more unrecognised mini-states. While humming the *Enthusiasts' March*, he added, 'We have to think of the bottom line.'

Ignoring him and his patriotic song, Alexandra then chirped, 'I'd like my name to be on a *European* passport.'

With another glass-cracking laugh, Nikoluk pulled himself upright in his chair. Pretending to be a border guard, he inspected her document and welcomed her into an imaginary, expanded European Union. 'Nikoluk, Alexandra…' he read aloud, then hesitated. He had forgotten her middle name. 'What is your patronymic again?' he asked his young wife.

For the first two decades of its existence Transnistria's leader, factory manager Smirnov, had maintained the guise of a working man. His suits had been tailored with peculiar, short rolled-up sleeves, a Lenin goatee beard added to enhance his presidential looks. None of his four election victories was recognised by the outside world. He fell from power when the Kremlin unexpectedly voiced its lack of confidence in him, and his challengers harnessed Facebook to campaign for change. In defeat Smirnov smashed his office, wailing at his aides, 'You said that I would win. You said that I was the winner.' His election slogan had been 'The Motherland is not for sale', a truth for the simple reason that it had already been sold out.

During his regency Smirnov had enriched himself, along with his family and favoured colleagues. His eldest son Vladimir had been head of the Customs Office. His younger son Oleg had been a presidential councillor and allied with the country's most powerful corporation, like Smirnov himself.

But after the election Smirnov went missing, maybe to a gated villa outside Odessa, or perhaps onto a bullet-proof mega-*yachtski* moored off Monte Carlo. In the days before his departure 90 per cent of the central bank's gold reserves vanished into secret accounts abroad. The incoming president found only $49,000 in the national kitty.

27

overleaf: Noul Neamț Monastery in Chitcani was founded in 1861 and closed by Soviet authorities from 1962 to 1989. To some commentators Transnistria's 1992 'Independence War' was staged by local Communists and Russian oligarchs so as to create a criminalised enclave for illegal activities.

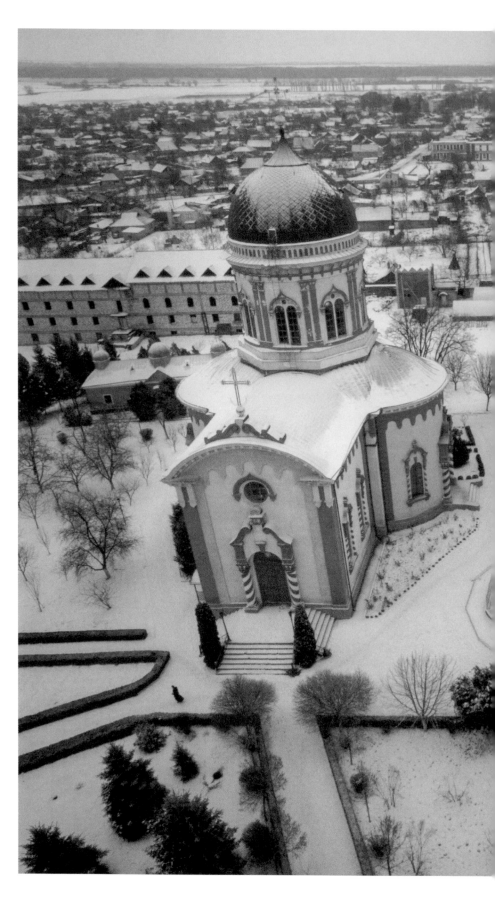

4

Big Brother

Beneath a sweeping blue arch crowned with a Sheriff yellow star,
a uniformed guard asked our business.

'Comrade, we are here to help to blaze the trail to the future,'
I told him.

On the seat beside me New Soviet Man rolled his eyes in
disbelief. 'Do not joke about dreams,' he warned me, with a wink.

The guard checked his list and directed us off the potholed
Tiraspol street and onto a Hollywood-slick paving stone drive.
We drove through the landscaped grounds, around the star-shaped
flower beds and manicured training fields towards the stadiums.
In front of a new five-star hotel, so much pride swelled in my host's
heart that again he started to sing, this time the national anthem
which praised the 'Republic of Freedom's gardens and factories,
settlements, fields and cities'.

'Our Slavic heart is big,' he enthused with extraordinary
emotion. 'We give all to that – and those – we love. We get hurt
of course, but it doesn't matter. A heart exists to beat and bleed.'

Sheriff's sports complex and football clubs are both the

'Citizens of the Soviet Union – strictly adhere to the
Constitution of the USSR, the Basic Law of our life.'

company's and country's boldest holding, built up over the last decade at a cost of more than $200 million. When filled to capacity the three FIFA-approved arenas seat one-tenth of Transnistria's entire population.

'Why football?' enthused Pyotr Lyalyuk, director of the complex, as we explored his oasis. 'Because football is the ambassador of peace. After the collapse of the Soviet Union, we at Sheriff decided to invest our money in the ambassador of peace.'

Lyalyuk introduced himself as Transnistria's former Criminal Police Chief. Like the company's founders, many Sheriff executives had first worked as intelligence officers or policemen. Behind him in the vast indoor hall, half a dozen teams of different ages practised at the nets.

'I oversaw the project from the very start,' recalled Lyalyuk with smooth self-esteem. 'I remember when there was nothing here but a simple field. Now we have built a kingdom for football.'

As we circled the hall Lyalyuk and his managers explained how Sheriff sponsored sports clubs in dozens of local kindergartens. Once a year the children and their families were invited to the complex. Company coaches selected the best players and offered them places at the Sheriff Football Academy. Over 400 boys were schooled there without charge. Children from out-of-town were given room and board. Boots and kit were also free.

'Thanks to our Club president Viktor Gushan, our director Mr. Lyalyuk and our sponsors, we can offer the boys a future in football, and put a smile on their faces,' said the Academy's principal, with a respectful bow toward Lyalyuk. 'This is the main purpose of the Club's work.'

The principal was a sincere and enthusiastic professional yet at the same time he radiated a certain caution, wary perhaps of saying the wrong thing, of being misunderstood, of the people who had power over his life. He parroted, 'Football is the most loved sport in the world.'

previous pages: Sheriff, the company that controls almost all profitable business in Transnistria, was founded by two former KGB officers. Its vast football enterprise is the company's largest holding, worth more than $200 million. Sheriff is considered to be the best-functioning institution in Transnistria, alongside the KGB.

As a result of its programme and investment, FC Sheriff Tiraspol has come to dominate football on both banks of the Dniester, winning every Transnistrian and Moldovan championship title for the last decade. The team twice won the Commonwealth of Independent States Cup and is now set on topping the European Champions Leagues. Graduates of the Academy have been sold to both European and Russian teams.

Nikoluk had told us that football was good business. 'Clubs train young players and sell them abroad for millions. No one does the business better than Sheriff. The future of Sheriff – and Transnistria – is beyond our borders.'

On an AstroTurf pitch New Soviet Man now added with pride that clubs such as Barcelona, and both Chelsea and Monaco FC which are owned by fellow oligarchs, were useful vehicles for money laundering. 'Business is like a car,' he assured me. 'It will not run itself except downhill.' He didn't go so far as to suggest that both FC Sheriff Tiraspol and the republic itself were 'a cash launderette'.

Transnistrians' dreams may be rich beyond measure but, with an average monthly income of $150, I wondered how such a costly sports complex could be afforded. I asked Lyalyuk, 'Where did the money come from?'

'Business,' he replied with a charming smile, before offering us cake and coffee in his private dining room. 'Please be my guests.'

Later over a glass of champagne we appreciated yet again the advantages of replacing the old idea of equality with the woolly notion of 'fairness'.

Sheriff was Nikoluk's 'Big Brother'. The omnipresent, private business had been founded by Viktor Gushan and Ilya Kazmaly, two KGB officers who had been Smirnov's 'sheriffs' during the independence war. But unlike Wild West lawmen, these sheriffs' intentions had not been only to fight crime. As well as the football teams and sports complex, their company had come to control a

bank, a chain of petrol stations, a mobile phone network, a couple of radio and television channels as well as the Mercedes-Benz franchise, two bread factories and the venerable KVINT distillery. Its dozen supermarkets offered huge selection – fresh mangos and raspberries in the middle of January, extra virgin olive oil from İzmir, salted Russian salmon, black caviar from the company farm at €1,200 per kilo – despite the moans of some locals that they could find nothing affordable on its shelves.

Of course Sheriff – the state within a non-state – wasn't the only party to have profited from Transnistria's non-existence. Over the 20 years alcohol, cigarettes and humans had been slipped across its porous borders. So many trailer loads of chicken were imported duty-free, then smuggled in secret to Ukraine, that on paper every Transnistrian ate 60 kilos of the meat per year. Some of the 40,000 tonnes of old Soviet weapons and ammunition stored near Cobasna had turned up in the Balkans, Chechnya and the Congo. Local weapons factories – so handy for the acquisition of hard currency according to my host – were said to have manufactured mines, grenade launchers and parts for Grad missiles destined for Iran (and not dissimilar to the SA-11 'Buk' thought to have brought down Malaysia Airlines flight MH17 in 2014). In the months before my journey a kilogram of radioactive Uranium-235 – a type of uranium that can be used in nuclear weapons – was seized in nearby Chişinău. Among its smugglers were two enterprising Transnistrians.

Business apart, the Kremlin also considers Transnistria to be of crucial geopolitical importance, straddling as it does its border with the EU and NATO. Canny Muscovites have used it to entrench their influence, for example with the vast Kuchurgan power station which supplies Transnistria, Moldova and much of Odessa. One year after its surprise sale to a Belgian shell company for a knock-down price, it was bought by Russia's state electricity producer RAO UES,

previous pages: On and off the pitch Sheriff – as well as all three of Transnistria's political parties – compete to see who can be the most enthusiastic supporters of Vladimir Putin.

netting the managers (some of whom were on the boards of both companies) about $100,000,000.

Sheriff's near monopoly had been protected by Smirnov. But as the home market was bled dry, Transnistria's indeterminate status slowed the company's growth. Future profit lay in trade with the West, whatever one's politics. With Sheriff's support an opposition party was formed, its young and charismatic leader challenging Smirnov's authority. Like at least half of all the Supreme Soviet deputies, he had served as a Sheriff manager at one time or other. It was he who replaced Smirnov as president.

5

Che Guevara High School of Political Leadership

Che Guevara lives in Transnistria. His portrait gazes out from the sunshine yellow banners of PRORIV: defiant, inspirational, iconic, and wildly out of place. The PRORIV (or 'Breakthrough') youth movement is – according to its glossy manifesto – 'like thunder, like a basin of icy water, like an avalanche that makes the world look at Transnistrian youth in a new way'. PRORIV's 'children of the sun' rally together against war and defeatists as well as epidemics, natural cataclysms and loneliness. Its ambition is 'eternal and indestructible union' with Russia, along with the overthrow of 'all the illusions of the modern world – capitalism, globalization, world market of goods and services, mania of consumption'. It also hopes to banish money.

'When I founded the movement, I wanted to find a symbol that was both romantic and revolutionary, a figure which meant independence both within Transnistria and abroad,' PRORIV's guru-cum-head teacher Dmitry Soin told us at his top-floor academy. 'I chose Che Guevara because kids think he's a cool guy.'

Around Soin perched a circle of spellbound disciples, their eyes

41

Katia Shvedul is PRORIV's editor and webmaster. Along with 'eternal and indestructible union' with Russia, PRORIV wants 'to end epidemics, natural cataclysms and loneliness'.

fixed on him in veneration. Aged 43, their shifty swami sported a bold blue tartan blazer and a ghost of a moustache. His dark brown hair was neatly trimmed. Once he had been a KGB officer, brandishing sword and shield for the Party. Now he was wanted by Interpol for murder.

'I've never accepted the idea of Transnistria as the front line between Russia and the Atlantic world,' the opposition parliamentarian assured us, preaching peace to his militant admirers. 'We must try to rid ourselves of this confrontational ideology,' he proclaimed, as I wondered how many Kalashnikovs were kept in the locked cupboard behind his desk.

In the chair beside me New Soviet Man was unexpectedly quiet.

'To be pro-Russian does not mean one has to be anti-Atlantic. Look at Moscow's example,' Soin went on. 'Everyone can see that the political elite are investing their money in European banks and business; that their wives shop in European shops. Transnistria is not the place where NATO tanks will be stopped, but rather a bridge between eastern and western Europe.' Like most of his countrymen, Soin also supported Moscow's 'example' of funding, arming and urging forward the violent insurgency against neighbouring Ukraine.

Across the hallway in his three-room Che Guevara High School of Political Leadership, other devotees learned how to prepare for 'spontaneous action'. They raised their arms in closed-fist salute and shouted 'Che!' and 'Breakthrough!' Elsewhere in the office the young fighters attended yoga classes beneath a poster of Soin in a loincloth in the lotus position.

'I start every day with the Tibetan Complexes,' he boasted, referring to the Five Tibetan Rites, an ancient system of exercises reputedly imported to southern California by a retired British army colonel. 'In the summer I like to perform them on the roof of our building overlooking Tiraspol. If all politicians thought in a yogic way, I believe there would be far fewer wars in the world.'

42

Dmitry Soin, founder and leader of the PRORIV party, admires politicians who have changed the face of nations: Luther, Calvin, Mahatma Gandhi and Stalin 'for the way he behaved towards Hitler. Of course I do not talk about his internal policies'. A former KGB officer, Soin is wanted by Interpol for murder.

The accolades seemed to swoon, among them tall Julia Zhukova, the attractive 24-year-old PRORIV chairwoman. Her predecessor, Alena Arshinova, recently joined the Coordinating Council of President Putin's Young Guard with 'superspy' Anna Chapman. While Soin searched for a video on his computer, Zhukova shared with me her views on patriotism, destiny and 'the country in which we want to live'. She was a qualified anaesthetist, both thoughtful and grateful for something – anything – to believe in. Like the dusty Communist Oleg Khorzhan, her zealous nationalism was a response to a sense of groundlessness. She clung to a dream of life under Moscow's guidance, even though Russia was 500 miles away.

Zhukova also had a tendency to stand unexpectedly close to a visitor, engendering a feeling of intimacy; not exactly a 'honey trap' but rather a calculated and disarming near-embrace. She'd learned the technique well at the Che Guevara School.

'Look at how we are treated by the authorities,' interrupted Soin, swinging the screen towards me. On his computer a local PRORIV rally was seen to be attacked by 'thugs from the Militia'.

'Look what they do to an innocent photographer,' he cried.

In the staged film clip a teenage woman stepped forward and on cue her camera was snatched from her hands. Yet the 'thugs' ignored the video camera which continued recording the scene.

'Our website has also been attacked,' Soin went on, paranoid of the machinations of Transnistria's old and new president alike. 'Our electricity supply was disconnected for a time. Yesterday at the Ukrainian border the guards tried to search my car, as a form of intimidation. I refused to comply and they held me up for half an hour.'

Soin did not doubt that – as a member of the Supreme Soviet – he should be exempt from import regulations, that he is above the law. He told me that he admired politicians who had changed the face of nations: Luther, Calvin and Mahatma Gandhi.

46

previous pages: In the capital Tiraspol, PRORIV shares office space and dreams with the Che Guevara High School of Political Leadership. A cleaner sweeps up after a yoga class beneath a poster of Soin dressed in a loincloth in the lotus position.

'Plus Stalin for the way he behaved towards Hitler. Of course I do not talk about his internal policies.'

He also did not talk about Interpol's 'inconvenient' murder allegations. Nor did he mention his involvement in a 2005 attempt to sell an armed Alazan missile to an undercover British *Sunday Times* journalist for $200,000. In the yawning emptiness behind his babble of words, I sensed New Soviet Man's brief, unexpected pang of self-doubt. Business is business, and doubt is the enemy of success, but we both wondered to what sort of future a man like Soin would lead Transnistria?

According to its manifesto, PRORIV didn't define people by nationality, race or religion but by an *Übermensch* philosophy of 'those who are ready for self-perfection, and those who will always stay at the level of biological existence'. Through political action PRORIV aimed to 'form a new Man'.

'Another New Soviet Man?' I asked the seer of Transnistria's 'children of the sun'.

'All my life I have been a socialist but I also have anti-Communist feelings,' he replied beneath a yellow portrait of the Marxist Che Guevara. 'I really hope that one day all the old monuments will be put away in a Museum of Socialist History.'

'And replaced by what?' I asked, now doubly suspicious.

'Replaced by monuments to individuals who have helped society.'

'No more icons?'

'There should be fewer idols,' said Soin with a smug smile, knotting himself in contradictions.

Perhaps he imagined his own statue on a plinth in Tiraspol's 'Breakthrough' Square. If so, it was not to be. Not long after our meeting, he fled to the newly formed Republic of Crimea to avoid arrest and the courts ordered the closure of PRORIV. The new regime didn't seem to tolerate his kind of opposition, no matter how inept.

'Let us strengthen the powerful, unbeatable union
of the three basic revolutionary forces of our time
– peaceful socialism, the international proletariat,
and the national liberation movement!'

6

In Praise of Propaganda

Where does a faithful man turn when – in a moment of weakness – he loses sight of social biologic ideals? How does he uphold the struggle for equality, peace and friendship between all peoples, yet not resist the temptation of easy money or, say, the gift of a Gulfstream *bizjet*?

Beyond the offices of the rich and powerful, fear has become a habit in Transnistria. In dirt poor Dzerzhinsky, a village named after the founder of the KGB, collective farm workers count their $15 'Putin pension', praise the Kremlin and keep their complaints to themselves. In a nearby Palace of Culture ethnic Moldovan students play safe, sandwiching their traditional dances between performances of the Russian 'Chunga Changa' and Michael Jackson's 'Thriller'. At the Noul Neamţ Monastery in Chitcani, Abbot Father Pasii lowered his voice to tell me, 'People have acquired the habit of fear. Please understand that it has only been a short time since President Shevchuk's election, and a short time is not 20 years. It will take time to change the old ways of thinking.' New Soviet Man was even more succinct. 'Freedom for the pike means death for the

overleaf: In front of the Supreme Soviet looms an enormous statue of Lenin, his granite cape flying out behind him like that of a superhero. The breakaway republic has its own government, currency and army yet remains unrecognised by any sovereign nation, Russia included.

minnows,' he told me.

Within hours of Shevchuk's December victory, dozens of craggy bureaucrats and hoary *nomenklatura* were replaced by 'Shev's chicks'. His drop-dead gorgeous Foreign Minister Nina Shtanski was 34. The new Minister of Justice Maria Melnik had just marked her 30th birthday. Alena Shulga, Minister for Economic Development, was 32. The new director of national television Irina Dementieva was a rosy-cheeked 28. In government they were soon joined by Minister of Finance Elena Girzhul, 34, and Tatyana Skrypnik, the 28-year-old Minister of Health. Apart from utilising these impeccable young women's bright vitality and expertise, the president's intention was to 'sex up' the republic's image abroad, letting their sheen obscure the shadows of the past.

On the 17th floor of a residential block, Irina Dementieva's office overlooked Tiraspol's snow-covered east end. On the floor below was her competitor TSB – 'Television of Free Choice' – owned by Sheriff. In her job for just a few days, Dementieva seemed to have found time only to hang the Transnistrian crest.

She made us coffee herself, because the former director's secretary didn't offer to do it, and talked about how her four-man team planned to 'collaborate' with the station's 180 employees to 'modernise' their ways of thinking. I had imagined that her job would be to transform the dutiful trumpet of the Party into a kind of big band advocate of pluralism. Instead she stuck to the old song sheet, talking of the need for 'productive and constructive work' and passing us a plate of chocolate biscuits.

'Long live the revolution!' applauded New Soviet Man, politely refusing her offering as he preferred Pierre Marcolini Belgian macaroons. 'What's the point of change for change's sake, unless there's profit in it?' he went on, chatting easily with Dementieva about responsible collaboration between media and government, as well as children's programming.

53

Irina Dementieva, 28, is the new director of the
First Republican Channel. 'Transnistria is
unique in being the only country in the world
not to have recognised the collapse of the Soviet
Union,' said her colleague. 'This is a joke.'

Suddenly – in a cheeky and provocative manner – I interrupted them to ask what she would do if Putin's press secretary called with a request to cut a controversial programme. At that moment her telephone rang and Dementieva all but jumped out of her chair, her arched eyebrows rising high above her designer glasses.

Comrades, we laughed and laughed.

There and then we both admitted to Dementieva that we both could be sentimental about the old Soviet certainties: the reassuring red star, the puffed-up busts of Lenin, the empty supermarket shelves. After all, it would be unfeeling not to long for that which once was, or nearly was.

I then asked her – as director of national television – to explain why so many symbols from those days were retained in Transnistria.

'It is our heritage,' volunteered her secretary.

'But some outsiders now consider them to be ... hollow,' I ventured, noting that no other European country still flies a national flag depicting the hammer and sickle.

'We are not competent to change the symbols,' Dementieva explained, meaning she did not have the authority.

'Why tease a growling dog?' said the secretary, firmly ending the conversation.

Lenin once said that film – and by extension both television and the internet – was the state's most powerful weapon. I also recalled that propaganda relieves the individual from the burden of independent thinking.

In the turmoil of heart and mind neither of us slept that night; me for turning over and over in my head the meaning of 'the scientific certainty of Communism', and my host because of a clerical error in his Credit Suisse bank statement. Sometime after midnight we turned on the television, and saw ourselves 'interviewed' on the First Republican Channel. We hadn't noticed any cameras in Dementieva's office.

Some of the bloodiest battles of the Second World War were fought on Transnistrian soil, stories of which are perpetrated in national mythology to bolster the call for ongoing individual sacrifice. Comrades! Be ever watchful! The Fascists are at the gate!

7

'To the bottom, Comrade!'

At the sharp end of the revolution New Soviet Woman strode alongside New Soviet Man. She was a proud and sober Communist citizen, a full-time worker, a wife and a mother, strong in body and resolve, freed forever from the double shackles of patriarchy and capitalism. Marx, Lenin and Stalin all spoke of her role in the triumphant realisation of Socialism. Unfortunately they kept stum on the lure of leopard-spot baby-dolls and high-potency alcohol.

Transnistrian women dress to shock. In summer they wear scant miniskirts and high heels. In winter they wrap themselves in long winter coats, the deep fur-lined hoods enhancing the face like a picture frame.

'I never go out of the house without my make-up,' said Marina Kereeva, a striking 50-something journalist and survivor: blonde, effervescent, with sharp, angular features and metallic cherry lipstick. 'It's the southern mentality to show our sunshine joy for life.'

On the pavement New Soviet Man embraced her in a great bear hug. '*Tovarish* Marina, every time we meet you become more beautiful,' he said, charming her with a maxim on the enduring

'Long live Soviet women, fervent patriots, active participants in the labour and social life! Honour and praise to mothers, warmly giving their hearts to the education of their children, the future builders of Communism!'

beauty of Russian women. *Замороженное мясо сохраняется дольше*. Frozen meat keeps longer. For her part Marina noticed his cologne, made for him at Le Labo in New York.

Marina was an old acquaintance of my host, a high-stakes 'fixer' who introduced foreign visitors to government ministers, Sheriff executives and invitation-only pole dancing clubs, guiding them between the proletariat dream and competing restaurants offering 'Bizness Lunch' specials. Often after championing the advances of the glorious republic, she felt at a loose end so we invited her to join us at KVINT, the Tiraspol distillery that was a source of national pride.

In the Bentley Marina told us a little of her life story. As a child she had wanted to dance for the Bolshoi, she said. Her mother had rewarded every ballet lesson with a piece of cake. Her passion for dance morphed into an appetite for treacle sponge. Soon she became overweight and lost her chance. The failure fired her determination and she starved herself back into shape, too late to be a dancer but soon enough to win her her very own New Soviet Man.

'He was a soldier in the Red Army with big eyes, black hair, so strong, and so often away from home. When he came on leave, our meetings were a celebration.'

The story warmed my heart, until Marina said that when he left the army and they moved in together, she discovered they were very different people. Like many former soldiers he found himself uneasy in civilian life, without a role or work, and apt to use his fists.

'We either argued or sat in silence. It wasn't a lucky marriage.'

In her need for her own life Marina joined the then new First Republican Channel, landing a position in the news room. Her unemployed husband felt both shamed and emasculated by her independence, calling her 'a shitty intellectual' and refusing to either watch her programmes or read her articles.

'He kept trying to change me, and the more he tried the stronger I became.'

He turned to drink and had affairs. After 19 years of marriage Marina divorced him. Yet as he couldn't find work she – with her soft heart – took on a second and then a third job to support both him and their daughters. Nevertheless the family began to starve. When a local businessman thanked her for a favour with a leg of pork, her girls cried, 'The hungry days are over! The hungry days are over!'

Marina became press officer of the Supreme Soviet, worked evenings at a local paper and presented a weekend money programme on Pridnestrovie Radio. At each job she wrote under a different name. When the Supreme Soviet learned about her moonlighting and ordered her to stop, she refused and quit, with no pension, no savings, no health cover. At the same time her husband – now a chronic alcoholic – tripped in his apartment, hit his head and died.

'Drink not only changed me and the children, it ended his life. I buried him in the cemetery near to my apartment. I am a widow.'

Marina pulled a fuchsia compact from her bag, checked her make-up and hair, made small adjustments to her appearance. Her mobile rang and she answered it with a curt 'Da.' When she made a call her fingers – tipped with chocolate brown varnish – attacked the keypad like talons.

Glory to the unflagging productivity of the Motherland's wine and spirit workers! Every year the triumphant KVINT produces 20,000,000 bottles of alcohol. Its 30 brands of brandy, and 40 types of vodka, whisky, calvados and dessert wine are exported to countries as far afield as Uruguay and Papua New Guinea. Every noble labourer treasures an unopened bottle for guests, although considerate visitors always choose to drink any cheaper homemade brew on offer. No prizes for guessing the owner of the distillery.

'It was like a dream come true when Sheriff bought KVINT,' the stocky and earnest Master of the Cellar Elena Gontsa told us. 'Suddenly we could afford the best European processing equipment. We could expand our vineyards. We could invest in French vines

grafted on to frost-resistant American roots: Chardonnay, Sauvignon, Merlot. The company even pays for us to travel abroad for professional training.'

Gontsa – like all KVINT workers and other servants of the conglomerate – receives job security and reduced price football tickets. The on-site Sheriff supermarket gives employees a ten per cent discount. At its health clinic, a gynaecologist and lung specialist work alongside seven other medics to serve its 750 employees. Medical care is free. A job with Sheriff is a job for life.

'There used to be something called Communism,' said Gontsa, with a twinkle in her eye. 'Sheriff has ensured that its finest qualities will never be lost.'

Heavy drinking is a tradition in the Slavic world. In an attempt to minimise its effect, Mikhail Gorbachev instituted a large-scale anti-alcohol campaign in 1985: closing factory bars, outlawing the sale of drink before 2pm, banning it at official functions. Among his predecessors were many legendary drinkers, including General Secretaries Brezhnev and Chernenko who is thought to have died from cirrhosis. Almost immediately the campaign – backed by the All-Union Voluntary Society for the Struggle for Sobriety – led to an increase in life expectancy as well as a bloom of pregnancies.

But then illicit production in a million Communist kitchens undermined the Prohibition campaign, leading to a massive rise in consumption. Over the next few years both mortality and childbirth in the old USSR dropped by a factor so dramatic as to be unprecedented anywhere in the world in peacetime.

In the bottling plant women in white smocks and tall chef-like hats worked in teams pasting labels onto the bottles. Warehousemen carried the filled cases away to trucks.

'I became a vintner because of my father's advice,' Gontsa volunteered, leading us through warehouses heady with the smell of yeast and alcohol. 'When I finished school he said to me,

62

previous pages: KVINT cognac – 'the beverage that gives pleasure' – is the nowhereland's most important legal export, helping to slow the region's slide towards recession. Nevertheless, capital flight out of Russia and its satellites doubled in 2014, helping to fuel the property boom in London and on the Côte d'Azur.

"Transnistria will always need winemakers." I always listened to my father.'

A long oak table lined with 40 chairs stretched to the far end of the degustation room. At its head over the next two hours Gontsa guided us back in time, first with a taste of 15-year-old 'Tiraspol' brandy, which had been laid down in oak barrels when the republic was still young, and then with 25-year-old 'Victoria' XO which had been an immature *eau-de-vie* at the time of the fall of the Berlin Wall. Next came 40-year-old 'Suvorov', named after the eighteenth-century Russian general and distilled from grapes which had grown while America was at war in Vietnam.

KVINT's 50-year-old 'Prince Wittgenstein' followed, a brandy which dated from the year that Kennedy had been in the White House, Khrushchev in the Kremlin and British defence minister John Profumo in bed with Christine Keeler, the call girl who he'd shared with a Russian agent. According to Gontsa, each of the cut-crystal bottles with leather labels and hand-painted miniature of the prince sold for $2,500. The first two numbered bottles of the limited edition – No. 1 and No. 2 – had been sent to Russian leaders Putin and Medvedev.

'Which one of them received No. 1?' asked New Soviet Man, but Gontsa responded by wagging her finger at him.

'Light white grapes with neutral aroma and high acidity are best for cognac,' she said instead, explaining the process of double distillation, and the ageing in oak to give aroma and colour. 'Our barrels – some as old as 50 years – used to be imported from France and Spain. Now they come from Nagorno-Karabakh.'

Workers of Transnistria! Struggle for the further development and strengthening of our progressive alcohol industry!

Together we sampled a final mouthful of amber 'Solnechny' which our host explained had first been produced in 1967 to mark the 50th anniversary of the Great Russian Revolution.

'*Solnechny* means "sunny" as if to herald a "sunny" Soviet future,' she said.

The good spirit quickly went to my head. In jest I related to my fair companions a Polish sailor's anti-Soviet toast from the old days. The Pole had raised his glass and called out to his compatriots' surprise, 'To the Red Fleet.' As they stared he had added, 'To the bottom' and drained his glass.

In the heavy silence I noticed Marina's downcast expression and said, 'It was a joke, Comrade Marina.'

The cherry-lipped New Soviet Widow tensed her chocolate brown talons, put on her coldest smile and declared with profound insincerity, 'I have such a soft spot in my heart for KVINT.'

64

For years, Russia has supported Transnistria: buying its alcohol, gifting it gas, subsidising its pension fund. As a Bolshevik, Vladimir Putin knows that vast territories can be conquered without big armies, as was achieved in the Russian Revolution. KVINT's directors hope that one day he will visit their Tiraspol degustation room.

8

Cultural Dreamer

'Light is my religion,' said Sergey Panov, landscape artist, President of the Union of Transnistrian Painters and conforming non-conformist. 'All my life I've had a recurring dream. In it I am a child holding a mirror, reflecting sunbeams onto a white wall. It's my oldest, most moving memory. I always try to bring it – as my love of light – into my work.'

As a boy Sergey didn't dream of being a painter. He wanted to be a footballer. He practised from dawn until dusk in the yard of his old family home. 'I imagined that I was Pelé, and that the metal postbox was the goal. Every time I hit it, and knocked it off the wall, my grandmother yelled, "What are you doing, you parasite? Stop playing that bloody game."'

To escape her anger he retreated to his tree house, and started to draw. 'I climbed this very tree,' he said, pointing out of his studio window into a now rubble-strewn orchard. 'I looked out over the field and river, revelling in nature's beauty, and wondered how to share it with others.'

Panov – now aged 54 – smiled at the memory, his soft, expressive

'Activists of literature and art, cultural workers! Carry high the banner of the party and national character of Soviet art! Give your talent and craftsmanship to the service of the people, to the job of Communism; create works of art worthy of our great Motherland!'

mouth all but hidden behind his beard. His neat hair had turned grey. He said, 'When we were children, we thought we would live forever. Now that we understand the truth, I try to reach back to that dream world.'

Panov had been born in a two-century-old thatched house built by a refugee Cossack forefather. His high ceilinged, open studio now overlooked that same building as well as a muddy lane silted up with converted farmhouses, satellite dishes and filthy feral dogs.

'It took me a hundred steps to become an artist,' he said, pulling on his long earlobes, looking at his neatly trimmed finger nails. 'With every two steps forward I fell one step back.'

He began to learn his craft by copying Russian realist prints. When his grandmother saw his work she kicked away his football and marched him to the local art school. Perhaps she understood that the activists of art, like all cultural workers, had a duty to carry high the banner of the Party and national character of Soviet art. Or perhaps she simply wanted him out of the house.

Panov did try to give his talent to the service of the people, to the job of Communism. But after graduation his application to the St. Petersburg Academy was turned down, two years in a row. He then tried for Moscow, failing again to find a place. Next he moved to Kiev, but the most suitable course only took entrants every six years. Finally he won a place at the Minsk Academy, in part because he could answer questions about Marxism–Leninist theory.

'At the Academy I lived without rules,' said the cautious rebel. 'I always argued with my teachers, took none of them as my mentor and so felt myself to be a self-made artist. A true painter works from his soul, with every brushstroke,' he cried as if quoting from a handbook.

Panov experimented with portraiture, painted sombre miniatures of workers at the Minsk Automobile Factory but soon he realised that he needed light.

'My creative influences are Russian realism, French impressionism and the sun.'

He devoted himself to painting landscapes of the southern borderlands, creating bucolic oils of the springtime riverbanks, winter canals and the Black Sea. His cities rose in the far distance like fairy-tale towers of progress. Not a single nuclear power station or soot-belching rubber tyre factory intruded on the idyll.

'My Motherland is wherever the apricot trees are in flower. Maybe there is rubbish lying on the ground or a high-voltage electricity line blocking the view, but one does not see it in my paintings. I do not see this as an idealistic perspective.' He touched his heart and said, 'It is a vision that comes from my soul.'

His biggest patron had been a government minister, until ousted in the election and replaced by a 30-year-old model. The man had bought 13 paintings during the Smirnov years, ascribing meaning to every canvas, for example fancying waves crashing against a Crimean fortress to represent the erosive forces of liberalism. 'I die for this picture,' he had told the artist. 'Your political insight moves me beyond words.'

Around the studio stood stacks of frame timber and rolls of canvas. On his work bench were jugs of brushes, tubes of paint and pink squares of toilet paper, neatly torn and stacked for cleaning bristles. On the studio wall hung a guitar and a tuba, missing its valves and mouthpiece.

Panov opened a bottle of his wine, even though it was still morning, and reminisced about joining the Union of Transnistrian Painters. He told me that he'd become its director 'in an attempt to change it'.

'In the old days, painters who belonged to the Party lived off the state. It was easy to survive, if you went along with the crowd. Of course no true artistic development could take place in such an atmosphere.'

He sighed and went on, 'Unfortunately today we live in a hard market economy. I still despise artists who follow trends so as to buy themselves a comfortable life. I have only sold one big painting since the autumn.'

Panov's work had been exhibited at Tiraspol's National Gallery and the State Duma of the Russian Federation yet his income came only from the sale of small studies. He opened cupboards to show me hundreds of them, dragging them out of their stacks, standing them one atop the other on the easels. There were oils of the Danube Delta at Vilkova, of a picturesque bend in the Dniester near Kamenka, of the country's oldest tree. In all his works, in the bright, beloved southern light, his colours seemed strangely muted.

'You are running out of space,' I said.

'I am running out of money.'

In the afternoon, after we had finished the second bottle, Panov set to work. He started on the shadows, trying to give depth to his canvas. He painted with his knees bent, poised like a sprinter at the starting line, with left arm thrown back and his right hand holding the brush like a baton. At the sight of him touching colour to the canvas I wanted to cry out loud, 'Activists of literature and art! Create works of art worthy of our great Motherland!'

Wisely, I kept my mouth shut.

'I will tell you a big secret,' Panov said, mellowed by the wine. 'My paintings are the result of a scientific approach. You know Pushkin's imagined conversation between Mozart and Salieri? Salieri is trying to understand the nature of talent, and he admits to Mozart, "I dissect music like a corpse. I measure harmony by arithmetics." That is me,' Panov admitted.

In Pushkin's play Salieri, the patron saint of mediocrity, is so envious of Mozart's true genius that he tricks and tries to poison him.

'Talent has precise and concrete criteria,' said Panov, dipping his deep-set, hooded blue eyes. 'Genius does not.'

72

previous pages: Transnistria – like Ukraine – is vital to Moscow as a buffer against the West, and as a route for delivering energy to Europe that is the foundation of the Russian economy. When neighbouring Moldova applied to join the EU, the Kremlin blocked its wine exports and threatened to cut off the natural gas supply. One senior Russian official warned the Moldovans, 'We hope you will not freeze.'

He laid down his brush and – after a sad glance out the window toward his lost tree house – raised his glass in a toast to 'inspiration'. Behind him in a corner hung a rare self-portrait; his dark silhouette and the shadow of a grape vine cast upon the wall where – in a dream – he'd once seen sunbeams.

Later outside as we waited for his car, New Soviet Man admitted to me, 'I never wanted to be a footballer or an artist but I enjoy Mozart. For me the most fascinating art is being successful at business.' Instead of the Bentley, a new Mercedes stopped in front of us. As his driver opened the door, New Soviet Man asked him, 'Is this one of my cars? I don't remember buying an E-Class.'

9

Earthly Paradise

At the edge of the Ministry of Justice compound, in a low modern office building, was GUIN, the State Service for the Execution of Punishment. Above the portraits of 15 be-medalled, stone-faced officer-heroes were inscribed the words of Tsar Peter the Great. 'Prison is a Hell for which we need tough professionals who work with good heart and joy.'

In the dismal entrance hall I announced our arrival.

'The animals are too cold to be seen,' barked the desk clerk.

'We have permission from the Deputy Minister of the Interior,' volunteered Marina, showing him an official letter. We'd come alone to GUIN, our New Soviet Man having slipped away to Odessa for a few days for a massage. He said he needed to ease his tension.

The clerk checked his roster. He made a call. A guard appeared, and then another. After ten minutes the first guard called us to the barrier and growled, 'We don't give a damn what the Deputy Minister says. We take orders only from the Minister. This is a restricted area.'

'This is a zoo,' replied Marina.

For decades the sliver-thin republic had been a Bolshevik Costa

At the headquarters of Transnistria's prison service is a private zoo, with free-roaming anaconda, emu, turtles, hawks and horses. Two-legged inmates care for the animals as a reward for good behaviour.

del Sol for retiring military men. But rather than busy themselves improving their golf swing like their western counterparts, the superannuated Heroes of the Soviet Union chose instead to commandeer government ministries, launch military coups and even – in this case – create a private zoo.

General Nikolai Goncharenko was a recipient of the Order of the Red Banner for heroism in combat. In 1968 he had ridden a Red Army tank into Czechoslovakia to crush the Prague Spring. In 1991 in Riga his OMON Special Purpose Mobile Unit had rounded up Latvian 'freedom fighters'. When the Baltic states proclaimed their independence, Goncharenko and his colleagues took shelter in Transnistria, knowing they'd not be bothered by extradition treaties. Along with Vladimir Antyufeyev, the first Minister of Security, they had organised the loyal colony along military lines. Goncharenko had taken charge of the country's prison service. With hard discipline and no money he'd renovated Prison No. 1 in Glinoe, where the cells had previously provided as little as one square metre of living space per prisoner. He'd reduced incidents of tuberculosis at both Colony No. 2 and Colony No. 3. He believed – as Antyufeyev had stated – that Communism would be built using Stalin's methods, with the people 'acting as in 1945–47, when every action against Order was considered to be an offence against the State'.

As well as discipline, Goncharenko loved animals. Soon visiting delegations from Serbia, Abkhazia, South Ossetia and other fraternal nations had begun to indulge his passion: a turtle dove here, an anaconda there. In time he had dozens, and then hundreds, of creatures. In his enthusiasm for selfless collectivism, he ordered the construction of cages and corrals in GUIN's central courtyard. Beneath the ubiquitous portrait of Dzerzhinsky, Goncharenko enjoyed nothing more than petting a dove or discussing his ostrich's vitamin supplements. One bitter Transnistrian winter he even

previous pages: 'Long live the valiant Armed Forces of the USSR, standing on watch to guard the victories of October and the peaceful labour of the Soviet people!'

housed the Pogona desert dragon lizards in his dacha sauna, to save the poor beasts from freezing to death.

The General had moved on to new challenges but, with a call to the new Minister of Justice, Marina finally secured sufficient authority for us to visit his creation.

In the courtyard newly recruited prison officers in battle fatigues shovelled away the fallen snow with their riot shields. Around them flapped pheasants, swans and Mandarin ducks. A rasp of guinea fowl honked as 'Emma' the ostrich pecked at the frozen mud. In a dozen other enclosures were marmots, peacocks and Highland ponies. Pigeons and chickens were bred to feed the anaconda and four-metre python, which the keeper let slither along the ministry's long hallways when cleaning its cage. Across from them roosted a pair of spooning parrots, the female of whom had just laid eggs. Turtles dozed in the cellar.

The keeper Mikhail Yavitza managed the furred and feathered inmates' feed as well as the administration of antibiotics.

'The animals are here for the relaxation of the staff,' he explained, although the guards didn't look up when the hornbill squawked at their anti-riot exercise. 'In summertime the ponies pull a cart around the grounds for visiting kindergarten children.' He said that the General stopped by every few days to check on the animals but in keeping with the socialist spirit, 'He has no favourite. He loves them all equally.'

'Has any animal ever escaped?' I wondered.

'None,' replied the keeper before adding, 'Now would you like to see me feed a live chicken to the python?'

overleaf: At Tiraspol's central square stands a statue of Alexander Suvorov, the tsarist general who seized Transnistria for Russia in 1792. Today Moscow prefers to take countries from within, through subversion, criminal activities and indirect control of media outlets.

10

True to his Word

'The Red Army was my school of life,' said Nikolai Gorobetz, his silver teeth catching the sunlight. 'It taught me the value of discipline and individual labour. Above all in the army I learnt communication.'

'Communication?' I asked.

'I served as a political officer for 26 years. I watched over my soldiers. If I saw a fellow walking with his shoulders slumped, I talked to him. I asked, "What's the problem?" Maybe his mother was ill. Or he had girlfriend trouble. I took care of him. To do this, I needed to enter his heart. My job was to manage the human soul. That's what I mean by communication.'

Gorobetz was another retired Red Army officer. Born 62 years ago in Ukraine, he had attended military school in Minsk. He adored the city, not least because he had been 'something of a Casanova' and in love with a girl named Svetlana.

'Then my best friend was ordered to a post in Siberia. His wife threatened to divorce him if he accepted it. As I was single, I went instead of him. When Svetlana and I parted, I swore that I would

Nikolai Gorobetz, director of the Tiraspol Orphanage, with his wife Nina. The orphanage is home to 63 children, all under the age of seven, some of whom are disabled. 'We grow attached to them of course, but wouldn't you be happy to see that they have a new life?' asked Gorobetz, a retired Red Army Colonel.

never forget her,' he told me. 'I even promised to name my first daughter after her, so she would always be in my heart.'

But in Siberia Gorobetz met another woman, Nina, and married her. 'She was a real officer's wife. She was never afraid of obstacles. She followed me to Baikal, to Khabarovsk, to East Germany. Once when I forgot my winter coat, she posted it to me, along with a letter as long as a book. She also accepted that our first born was to be named after Svetlana.' He paused and smiled at the memory. 'Like I said, she was a real officer's wife.'

Gorobetz and Nina's first child was a boy.

'When we tried for a second kid, we watched the timing, followed the stars. You know, if you want to have a boy you have to – how should I say this? – put under the woman's backside some male symbol: a gas mask, a helmet or a bayonet for example.'

'And for a girl?'

'For a girl you just put a pillow under the woman and get on with it,' he explained with a shrug. 'So what happened? We had another boy. I never had a little girl to name Svetlana.'

When the Soviet Union broke apart, Gorobetz was offered a commission in the Ukrainian Army.

'But I turned it down. I had sworn my allegiance to the USSR and I was willing to give only one oath in my life.'

His final Red Army posting had been in Tiraspol. As he was reluctant to give up the apartment that had come with it, he decided to stay on. In the new republic he was appointed to Transnistria's Special Orphanage of the Republic.

'My heart ached when I first saw the children. I decided that, whatever it cost me, I would do everything possible for these dear, poor souls.'

As the animal-loving Goncharenko had done in the prison service, Gorobetz brought military rigour to another civilian institution, shaping the orphanage into a miniature moral society which demanded absolute loyalty to both authority and the group.

'Years ago in Minsk I went to a movie during my lunch break. In the middle of the show the military police had arrived and demanded to know why people were watching a film on a weekday, and not working for the common good. That's what I call discipline. That's what I call order.'

As we talked, half a dozen young, teenage women arrived carrying plastic bags of donated toys. They dropped their winter coats and I followed them down the corridor to an open, airy room filled with miniature chairs, low work tables and a new television. Christmas tinsel still hung from the ceiling like slivers of falling snow frozen in time. On sofas and atop wardrobes were dozens of squeaky hedgehogs. Neat ranks of cribs and cots lined the adjoining room.

The children jumped up to meet the visitors. They were pony- and pig-tailed, or crew cut, dressed in colourful tops and slippers and the teenagers took them in their arms, talked to them, gave them cuddly snakes and clockwork caterpillars. A child recited a Christmas poem from memory.

'What do you want most in your life?' one of the visitors asked her.

'I would like to go home to my mother,' she replied.

Most of the orphans had been abandoned, or taken from parents who are alcoholics, in prison or diagnosed as HIV-positive. Gorobetz's 63 children were all under the age of seven, some were disabled.

'I grew up in a large family, and our parents taught us to love each other and care for each other at every moment,' he said. 'That was my other training for this job.'

In the next ward, three-year-old Olesea had only a single, stumpy arm. Her parents – who Gorobetz said were wealthy – had given up their deformed baby at birth, and sued the hospital for failing to detect the defect during pregnancy.

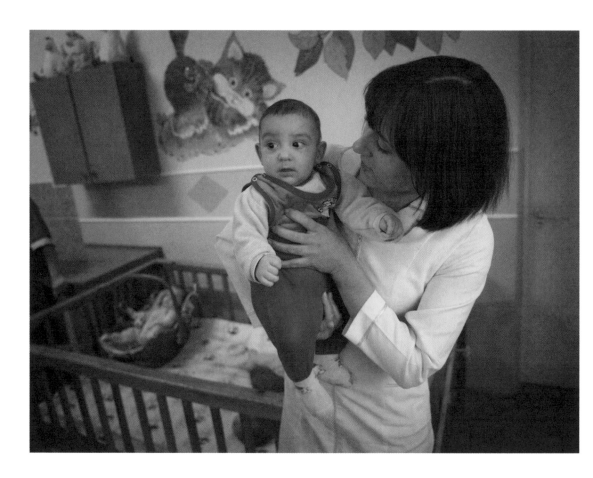

Most Transnistrians are nostalgic about Soviet days when 'people had jobs and pensions and there were no worries'. The republic's small elite class holds a different view.

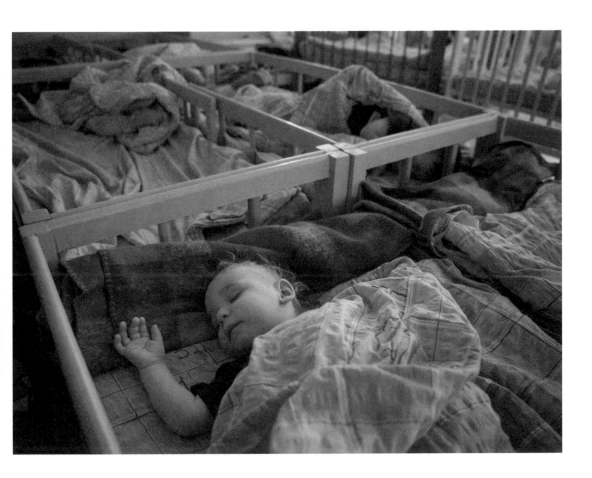

Many Western politicians are sleeping through the threat to the EU's eastern borders, wishing to maintain the steady supply of Russian energy and high-spending oligarchs to Europe. Fairy tales are also popular in Transnistria.

'Ladies, future mothers; look at this child,' called Gorobetz with feeling as he lifted Olesea into his arms. 'Take care what you are doing. Avoid drugs and do not become overexcited by alcohol. Observe the dangers of momentary love.'

After the visitors departed, the children trooped off for a communal toilet visit. Then they sat in silence on chairs beneath the television, their uniformed carer walking down the line, placing a single cheese puff in each open mouth, feeding them like a communion of obedient, colourful birds.

'These days the younger generation isn't interested in ideologies,' confessed Gorobetz when we returned to his office, an ancient warrior fretful of modern morality. 'All they care about is money, buying oranges cheaply in one place and selling them for profit in the next. To my mind these young people are lost because of the loss of the Party.'

He sighed and went on, 'I regret that Article Six – which stated that the Party must take a leading role in the affairs of the State – was excluded from the new Constitution. In the past, if there were failures, the Party had to answer for them. It was our responsibility. Now, I suppose, duty is a personal matter.'

He glanced over his shoulder and then asked, 'Would you like some wine? It's homemade by a neighbour.'

He slipped out to the kitchen, returning with two plastic bottles, one red and one white, as well as the ubiquitous unopened flask of KVINT brandy. He offered the brandy but poured the wine.

Every morning Gorobetz wakes at 05.30 and does 40 minutes' callisthenics before breakfast. On Tuesday, Thursday and Saturday evenings he swims at the city pool. On weekends he tends the orphanage garden, which supplies cabbages and potatoes for its kitchen.

'I need to stay fit so I can keep helping my 63 brave little soldiers,' he said. And sustain his children's utopia, I thought.

90

previous pages: Students from Tiraspol's No. 10 High School visit the orphanage, filmed by a television crew from the First Republican Channel. According to some foreign NGOs, as many as 60% of orphaned Transnistrian girls will be approached to become sex workers in later life.

As the light faded, the former Red Army officer kissed the hammer and sickle on the Transnistrian flag. He assured me that his soul was at peace and that he wanted for nothing. He and his wife had 'clothes and shoes, three pairs each'. He raised a glass to friendship and peace and said, 'My friend, my house is your house. My money is your money.' Then he grasped my hand and added, 'But my wife is my wife.'

'And what of Svetlana...?' I asked.

overleaf: 'Veterans of the Revolution, the war
and labour! Mentors of youth! Actively participate
in the education of the young generation in the
revolutionary, combat and working traditions of
the Soviet people!'

11

Factory

Transnistria once had secret arms factories, or so assert western rumour-mongers. The separatist republic was alleged to have hidden 14 weapon production units within legitimate works like Electromash and Pribor, owned by the Russian aero-engine manufacturer MMPP Salut. Like much of the country's industrial landscape, the buildings appeared grey and rusted, and often seemed to be abandoned, until one noticed the new surveillance cameras and busy employees' parking lots. Only then did one understand why the rumour-mongers remain so vociferous.

Bendery straddles the Moldovan border. The town's main employer is Moldavcabel. The company has also been named as a secret weapons maker.

'Here in Bendery we have worked, we are working and we will work,' said Yunis Ragimov. 'No financial crisis, no collapse of the Euro, no raw material inflation will stop us.'

Ragimov, 50, was Moldavcabel's general director. A dynamic and likeable man, he had been born in Armenia, educated in Azerbaijan and could crack jokes in five languages.

'Peoples of the world! Decisively speak out against the production of the neutron bomb! The design and production of new types of weapons of mass destruction must be halted!'

'Before we begin let me tell you that I served in Afghanistan,' he said in mock seriousness. He knew why New Soviet Man and I had come to Bendery. 'So be aware that the KGB may be listening to our every word,' he jested, reminding us of Stalin's dictate that gaiety was the most outstanding feature of the Soviet Union.

His factory had been founded in 1958. At its peak it had employed 2,500 people and supplied the electrical windings for many of the USSR's small motors: washing machines, television tubes, T-62 battle tank starter engines. Later it began producing cable conductors for generators.

Ragimov became its director in 2003 when a Saint Petersburg conglomerate bought the vast plant for US $1.7 million, about the cost of a single Tomahawk cruise missile. He slashed employee numbers to less than 500. He doubled productivity, then doubled it again, sending exports to Romania, Slovakia and the Baltic States as well as Russia.

'Sevcabel's acquisition has enabled us to be part of a big family, bringing us access to more markets,' he said. He had curly black hair, a wide moustache and lashes so dark that his eyes appeared to be rimmed with kohl. 'Now we need new investment. We're operating almost at zero revenue, bled white by competition and the lack of recognition. The United States and the EU want to keep us down. They want to weaken us.' He added, 'For this reason I am sure Transnistria will be reunified in ten years.'

'With Moldova?' I asked.

He shook his head. 'With Ukraine, Belarus and Kazakhstan.' He gestured toward the nearby border. 'Moldova is our neighbour. If you live in a block of flats and have bad neighbours you can move. We don't have that option.'

Had Moldova concocted the slanderous stories about weapons production, as Ragimov and others maintained? Or had a tipsy oligarch

98

previous pages: Moldavcabel – owned by the Russian conglomerate Sevcabel – is one of the biggest manufacturers in Transnistria. Its painting 'Day of Energy – 24 December 1918' celebrates Lenin's plan to electrify the Soviet Union.

At the Bendery cable factory 'heritage equipment'
– installed in Soviet times – has produced cable for
toasters, tanks and the generators at Iran's Bushehr
nuclear power station.

simply been bragging after too many Moscow Mules? Certainly the rumours had poisoned relations across the two banks of the Dniester.

'When two people freely choose to marry, their union is likely to be a success. If there is no free will, then the marriage will end in divorce. If Transnistria and Moldova got back together, it would be like Afghanistan. There will never be reunification with Transnistria and Moldova. That is the will of the people.'

Outside it had begun to snow, the flakes settling on backs and hats, hiding the horizon beneath a white blanket. An industrial graveyard of disused rail lines and rusted gantry cranes loomed out of the pallid air. Blocks of faded buildings appeared abandoned. Idle loading areas were knee-deep in pale drifts. New Soviet Man ventured that the location was ideal for an enterprise zone. 'I am hot on the potential of asset stripping,' he told me.

Inside one of the three accessible warehouses, pot plants drooped around 'heritage equipment' which had been installed in Soviet times and still made winding wires for generators. A stout worker tended the machine which had produced the cable for Iran's Bushehr nuclear power station. At a wooden OTK desk another woman in a pink woolly hat monitored quality control in a cloth-bound ledger.

Next door serpents of cable snaked across the floor, over painted white lines which defined the position of the humming machines, beneath a portrait of Lenin. Along the lines men wheeled spools of wire, working in eight-hour shifts, earning $350 per month.

At Moldavcabel I saw no sign of landmines, missile launchers or AK-47 ammunition production lines. Nothing apart from *draniki* potato pancakes seemed to be hidden in the staff canteen. Nor did I spot any sign of Aerocom or Jet Line, freight airlines which New Soviet Man said had landed regularly for 'technical reasons' at nearby Tiraspol on their way to Africa. Both carriers had been controlled by Viktor Bout, the enterprising arms smuggler and convicted

previous pages: Armaments production and illegal weapons trafficking are rumoured to be the largest source of revenue for the region's elite. Many Russian nationalists – including President Putin – are convinced that the West wants to destroy the Russian Federation, consigning it to history like the USSR.

'merchant of death' who – according to the British SIS – had often visited Transnistria.

Back in the administration block in a coloured glass mosaic, three Soviet cosmonauts circled the Earth, held together on their spacewalk by Bendery cable. On a concrete wall beyond them rose the words: 'Transnistria will live on!'

As we shook hands to leave, Ragimov joked, 'So you see, we have no secret weapons plant here.'

Neither New Soviet Man nor I wondered if we'd come to the wrong place.

12

I Believe in Miracles

Overnight the snow iced the orchards and fields on either side of the north highway. Once, summer corn and buckwheat had grown alongside the arrow-straight, three-lane highway. But at the end of January the shells of deserted houses looked colder than Siberian iceboxes. At a dirt side road a statue of an heroic farmer, forever clutching a sheaf of wheat to her swelling breasts, guarded the entrance to the abandoned Dnestrovsky collective farm. Along its rutted street grandmothers towed home churns of well water on sleighs. Their daughters sold pickled mushrooms in lilac-edged houses with corrugated roofs. The only man around was a traffic policeman stopping Ladas, checking papers, asking the drivers to breathe on him to prove they'd not been drinking. Transnistria seemed to be a place from which many had escaped, which many miss, and where those left behind try to build a normal life.

'The story I am about to tell you is absolutely true,' insisted Tatiana Kushnir, the effervescent, 39-year-old manager of the Kamenka Sanatorium. 'When I was a little girl, a Moscow couple came to Kamenka every summer to rent the dacha next door. We

In Soviet times the Kamenka sanatorium was the finest *Kurhaus* in the USSR. Party members, trade union leaders and workers who'd won productivity competitions joined cosmonauts and cinema stars for its 26-day rest and health cure.

called them our *dachniki* – or weekenders – and they looked after me when my parents were at work. One day I read a fairy tale about a tree that grew shoes, which struck me as silly nonsense.

'"You don't believe in miracles?" the *dachniki* said to me. "Then plant one of your old shoes and water it for three days and see what happens."

'I did as I was told and three days later I woke up to find a new pair of pretty pink sandals hanging on a bush.' She laughed, the waves of joy rolling off her like seawater off a swimmer. 'I've believed in miracles since that day.'

Tatiana seemed to be charged with a magnetic physicality. She talked so quickly that I could hardly keep up with her. Her forefathers came from Poland, she told me with a sparking touch on my arm. Her mother was a professional cook. Her father had played the trumpet. She grew up on the steep slopes that rise above Kamenka, among the vine terraces, overlooking the Dniester.

'I am in love with this land,' she said, gesturing towards the white cliffs which clasped the town at their base. 'Everyone who comes to Kamenka senses its aura, realises that it is unlike anywhere else in the world. We say that the cliffs hide us from time. Since the destruction of the Soviet Union, our out-of-time place has become even more precious to us.'

Kamenka *was* special. The writer Isaak Babel had rhapsodised about its watermelons. Vladimir Nabokov had spent his childhood summers exploring the hills and watching slender young girls bathe in the river. In the early nineteenth century the Tsar had gifted the land to Ludwig Peter Wittgenstein, the German-born prince who had saved Saint Petersburg from Napoleon. His descendants had terraced the sheltered slopes, importing vines and vintners from family estates on the Rhine, coming to produce the finest wine in the region. Grapes from the vines were later used by KVINT.

The protected bank seemed to focus emotional warmth as

much as sunshine. The natural spa waters enhanced its healthy reputation as did the building of a *Kurhaus* in 1890. In Soviet times its sanatorium was considered the most blessed in the USSR. Champion workers joined Party members, trade union leaders and movie stars for the 26-day grape-juice-and-wine cure. Its treatment programmes, its grounds, even its herb-lined walkways were designed by the Ministry of Sanatoriums in Moscow. In those halcyon days 600 guests lived behind its high walls, in rooms so full that staff slept in offices and on therapy tables.

'It was a city within a city,' recalled Tatiana, crackling with energy. 'When my sister and I snuck into the Saturday evening dances, it was like a dream!'

After graduation Tatiana found a job at the sanatorium, working her way up to the position of manager. Her sister took charge of the kitchen. At breakneck speed she led me between the treatment rooms, explaining the theories of colon hydrotherapy and magnetic resonance cures. 'We offer leech bleeding to strengthen the immune system, vacuum gradient therapy for deformed spines as well as intestinal irrigation,' she bubbled. 'And one must not forget our famous herbal enemas.' She encouraged me to drink an 'oxygen cocktail' of apple juice frothed with compressed gas then forced on me handfuls of delicious, local walnuts. 'One must eat walnuts for the brain. They are shaped like the brain.'

In the enormous dining room, its walls lined by full-length mirrors and a picture window overlooking the river, her sickly clientele picked at boiled chicken and assured each other how much better they felt. They appeared to be in shock, perhaps because their bills had now to be paid in dollars.

'Last summer my oldest friend came home from abroad,' said Tatiana as she finished her borscht. 'All she wanted to do was to pick a pear from her family's tree and bite into it. I'd cooked for days before her arrival and she told me, "Your dishes are delicious but

overleaf: Today the sanatorium is renowned for its special juice and wine cures as well as its spa water. Local apple juice frothed with oxygen and served with walnuts is said to improve brain function. Only dollar-paying guests are now accepted for treatment.

Kamenka's fruit is the best food in the world." Look!' said Tatiana suddenly, pointing out the window and at the cloudless winter sky. 'Snow geese. It is another miracle.'

After lunch I was hurried past a long mural of political, military and medical heroes to meet the sanatorium director.

'There are many stories of people being cured of their ailments,' droned Ivan Bystrov who was as dull and grey as Tatiana was bright. 'I remember a woman who suffered from arthritis. After three weeks with us she put down her stick and started to walk.'

'It was *amazing*,' sparkled Tatiana. 'Her stick is hanging on my office wall.'

Bystrov had served as an officer–doctor in the Far East. On his desk was a copy of *Pravda*. The day we met marked the 35th anniversary of his starting work at the centre.

'Many people forget their complaints by the time they leave us,' he said without a smile. 'But for the sanatorium to survive we need political stability in Transnistria. Some foreign clients have stopped visiting us. We depend on politicians to alleviate their fear. We need more people to come to Kamenka.'

Later at the gate, Tatiana unexpectedly embraced me. Behind her, a veneer of new aluminium panels covered the crumbling concrete buildings.

'You must promise to return to Kamenka,' she gushed, adding with a sudden tight smile that she was divorced, had no children, and lived at home with her grandmother. 'Then I will take you to my house and we will cook outdoors and drink red wine, which is good for the haemoglobin.'

'And look for the shoe tree?' I asked her.

'It is still there,' she insisted, grabbing my hand. 'I tell you, there is much for you to discover in this truly miracle land.'

The nine reasons why tourists visit Transnistria include 'an abundance of fruit and vegetables' and 'KVINT cognac at wholesale prices'. To perpetuate the division between it and its estranged western half, the republic's tourist board also declares, 'Compared to Moldova, Transnistria is like the Riviera.'

13

Freedom from Fear

'Fear?' said Nina Shtanski, as surprised as I was myself by the directness of my question.

Time and again on my journey people had spoken to me of fear, looking over their shoulder, lowering their voice. In truth in the old USSR, neither New Soviet Man nor his fellows had been blindly loyal to the Party. They'd never been unthinking puppets marching in May Day parades. All had known about the gulags, dreaded the pre-dawn knock on the door, developed a taste for twice-reheated cabbage *shchi*. After 1989 I'd thought that fear – along with the old stereotypes – had been buried under the rubble of the Berlin Wall. Yet now I asked the elegant and astute new Foreign Minister (and Deputy Prime Minister) if that unpleasant emotion remained a habit in Transnistria.

'Over the last twenty years fear has become a habit in Pridnestrovie,' admitted Shtanski, forming her response with care, using her preferred name for the republic. 'Today our people are waiting for some sort of settlement, for a system of international guarantees.' The fullness of her lips and eyes was emphasised by her

Nina Shtanski, 34, ten days after her appointment as Foreign Minister of Pridnestrovien Moldavian Republic (the official name of Transnistria). After 20 years under President Smirnov, people voted for change. 'We feel the weight of expectation, and we feel that the people's expectations is too high.'

dark, chestnut fringe. Her tailored blazer and schoolgirl-length skirt accentuated her height. She folded her hands together and ventured that the only way to break the habit of fear was 'to find a solution to my country's unrecognised status'. She added, 'It is a frozen conflict but still it is a conflict with accumulating conflict potential. It is dangerous.'

Behind her the bookshelves were empty. In the hallway beyond, plasterers hacked back old walls, the detritus drumming down onto cardboard sheets cut from air conditioner boxes. Her office in central Tiraspol had once been a nursery. Outside its window stood her new Audi.

In the weeks since her appointment 34-year-old Shtanski's beauty – as well as her fresh and sharp intelligence – had transformed Transnistria's image abroad. Diplomats from Brussels, London, Budapest and Geneva were queuing up to stare at her across the ministry's broad boardroom table. At the same time she launched her personal PR campaign, on Facebook.

'Good morning, friends, countries, continents! Wishing you a great week! May the news only be good, the winter frosts only kind, and meetings warm!' she wrote soon after her appointment. Another of her daily posts read, 'Watching Eurovision. Those Swedes have really bowled me over!!!!! Cool!' Once she even ventured, 'People of Tiraspol! Tell me please where in Tiraspol is a good place to roller skate?'

Her candid, snappy posts – about her love of fashion, home baking and Magners Irish cider – and her astute comments on trade and political negotiations reversed the outmoded Cold War stereotypes, making the republic appear to be trendily modern. After the Munich Security Conference she revealed a passion for German marzipan. During a Foreign Office-sponsored trip to Northern Ireland she raved about *real* Irish Christmas trees. She told the world of her enthusiasm for Joe Cocker, Santana and Portishead.

114

Her 'likes' included Chanel, *Esquire* Russia and Vladimir Putin. She defended her post-graduate dissertation from Moscow's prestigious MGIMO Institute, the top school for diplomats and the like, then shared a favourite joke about a couple's conversation after a night of lovemaking, 'She: "My darling, shall we get married?" He: "Let's stay in touch."'

Her Facebook diplomacy disseminated information about Transnistria, wrapped in an attractive package, winning her more than 5,000 friends – a significant achievement given that the unrecognised state has no embassies and only scant resources to promote itself abroad. Of course her beauty also placed her in a vulnerable position, even as she herself exploited it.

'Dear FB friends! I really really ask you to stop sending me offended comments. For the 104th time I don't answer posts like "Hi, how are things?" or the even-more-original "What's up? Let's meet."'

Back at the ministry table Shtanski spoke to me of the 'black myths' spread in the West which portrayed Transnistria as a source of arms and drugs smuggling as well as a conduit for human trafficking. She said that this 'unrighteous image' had to be broken. Once, she – or at least her predecessors – might even have alluded to foreign powers perverting the destiny of the brave little state. I started to ask her about the triumphant dictatorship of the proletariat but the words sounded hollow in my ears.

As we both knew, boldness is needed to thaw the frozen conflict. Yet can the European Union ever recognise a republic founded by armed struggle, thereby setting a precedent for Basque, Flemish, even Northern Irish independence? At the same time can it continue to treat Transnistria as a pariah, with its explosive alcohol and storehouses of decaying weapons? The human cost of Western inaction is incalculable. Moscow certainly wants to limit EU influence, as it does in Ukraine, holding on to Transnistria

by gifting it gas, drawing it into its Customs Union, using it as a political instrument for its own goals. Already Putin's infiltrators and provocateurs are in place, ready to take his 'masked warfare' over the Dniester, even to turn Moldova into the next battlefield.

Yet Shtanski and the other young politicians seemed to be sincere, confronting the economic situation, tackling corruption, even curtailing Sheriff's privileged position (President Shevchuk having fallen out with his former allies). But had their election really brought a regime change or only a change of leaders?

Shtanski answered me with the words, 'There has been a change of leader, and the new leader campaigned by offering changes to the principles of state administration. The people voted for him. The intention is to justify their trust.'

Transnistria's people are bound together by a shared Soviet identity, she emphasised. Over coffee she recalled a story about her daughter. One day her first grade teacher had begun a discussion about ethnic diversity, explaining to the class that Russians, Ukrainians and Moldovans lived together in harmony and equal numbers in the republic. The teacher then asked the children to stand up and state their ethnicity. One by one the children announced with pride, 'I am Pridnestrovian.'

'Our children are like a mirror,' Shtanski told me. 'This is national identity over ethnicity, and this fact will help us to solve common problems. Together we can build a common place.'

Yet hasn't every attempt to create a safe place in the world been doomed to fail?

Beyond her office door the builders had stopped for their morning break. High heels clicked on the marble floors. A telephone rang with the tune *London Bridge is Falling Down*. A few hours earlier a grenade had exploded around the corner from the ministry, near to the home of the former KGB internal security boss. No one knew if it had been detonated by 'terrorists' or by the peeved old KGB boss

previous pages: Joblessness is endemic in Transnistria. In the last 20 years its population has shrunk by one half so that now every working person supports about seven unemployed. A pensioner supplements her tiny pension by selling onions and eggs from a pram near the Vienna Café in central Tiraspol.

himself, as a way of reminding the newcomers how quickly power can change hands.

At the end of our meeting I asked Shtanski about her duty – and that of her young colleagues – toward a people who were both fearful and hopeful, who watch their words whilst befriending her and the new president on Facebook.

'We feel the weight of expectation,' said Nina Shtanski with a smile at once beautiful and sad. 'And we feel that the people's expectations are too high.'

14

Our Glorious Future

..

'What is Transnistria? I've never heard of such a place,' said the
stranger, turning away from me, keeping his identity to himself.
'I don't believe in borders.'

Tashlyk is a town of 3,000 souls, half an hour's drive north of
Tiraspol. Its name means 'rocky place' in Turkish, so called by
the fifteenth-century settlers whose houses still squat on a low
embankment above the Dniester. But the Turks are long gone, along
with thousands of other villagers who've left to find work in Moscow,
Odessa and Verona. The state shop and wine co-op have shut. Every
other building seems deserted with windows broken and doors
closed by a twist of rusty wire or twine. Along the muddy street
a thin line of smoke rises from a single chimney. Turquoise paint
flakes onto a forgotten patio. Two wooden planks, set at right angles
to each other, overlook the flood plain. Once a seat for friends, they
too are now unoccupied.

On the hill above stands the Tashlyk Compulsory Educational
School. Its water comes from a well, not the mains. An outside toilet
block serves its 357 students and 43 teachers. There is no sports field

'Young men and women! Persistently educate
yourselves in communist convictions! Learn to live,
work and struggle as Leninists, as Communists!'

and only a partially built canteen building, on which work stopped two decades ago. The reason for its poverty is hard to understand, given that Tashlyk is represented in the Supreme Soviet by Ilya Kazmaly, the co-founder of Sheriff and one of the republic's richest men.

'We teach by the National Education Plan as prescribed by the Ministry: math, history, science and languages,' explained the school's headmistress who had gathered together half a dozen fellow teachers in the staff room. 'We work as prescribed, as ordered. If we disagree with the curriculum what, in truth, can we do about it? We hope for radical change in the system.'

'Change?' I said, wondering about the role of these mentors of youth, wondering at last who were the true heroes – and victims – in Transnistria. It was no surprise that New Soviet Man had decided not to accompany me to the school.

'Look out the window; the new school building has been under construction for 20 years,' I said. 'You don't have a canteen.'

The staff stayed silent.

'What about history?' I asked them. 'How do you teach your … glorious history?'

'Please bear in mind that this is a Moldovan school, and the majority of people in Tashlyk are Moldovan. So we are in the minority in Transnistria,' said another teacher who also asked not to be named. 'We use Soviet-era textbooks translated into Moldovan which, for example, talk about the Great 1917 Russian Revolution. I try to update them by presenting another point of view, moving from the old utopian ideals to so-called Developed Socialism. But I have no material for this, only my own experience.'

'And Stalin?' I questioned.

'The accepted view is that Joseph Stalin brought Soviet victory in the Second World War. Our textbooks – or "manuals" – do not mention the deportations, the gulags, the loss of the brightest

124

previous pages: Tiraspol is 800 miles from Moscow yet the breakaway republic has asked Russia to annex it like Crimea, and to create an 'access corridor' across Ukraine. Such a corridor would be unlikely to accommodate prams.

minds...' She took a deep breath, her voice full of emotion. 'I am only "entitled" to teach the unilateral presentation of the historical process.' She paused to consider her words. 'Anyway I know most children will move away from Tashlyk after graduation.'

Later I learned that a new history textbook had finally been commissioned, by President Putin himself. In it Russia's tsars and Communist leaders are to be presented as 'enlightened autocrats'. Stalin's famines, purges and mass deportations are explained as the 'unavoidable cost of Soviet modernisation'. No mention will be made of *new* New Soviet Man.

In a classroom, students worked in pairs at pale blue desks beneath the words 'Science is the torch of truth'. Most girls wore their hair long, plaited or secured with plastic clips and simple bows. Many hung silver crosses around their necks. The boys sported white shirts without logos or branding. Their heroes were footballers and actors: Ronaldo, Andrei Arshavin, Arnold Schwarzenegger. Vladimir, aged 14, wanted to be a businessman 'selling clothes and furniture'. The girls dreamed of being lawyers, designers or – in one case – a policewoman.

'I want to join the police when I graduate,' said 15-year-old Varvara.

'But there is only a militia in Transnistria.'

'In Russia,' she replied, as if it was obvious. 'This is my home but what could I do here? There is no work, no money. I have to go away.'

Non-stop emigration had reduced Tashlyk to a community of children and *babushkas*. Only five of the 43 teachers were under the age of 40. Most of their pupils lived either with their grandparents or alone in the family house, the neighbours keeping a watch on them while their parents laboured abroad. The situation is little better in the republic as a whole, its population halved in two decades. In 1995 the headmistress' husband moved to Moscow to be a driver. 'We don't know where all the time has gone,' she told me.

Over the centuries Transnistria has been Polish,
Ukrainian, Romanian and Russian. In 1892 one-
third of Kamenka's population – 2,902 souls – were
Jewish. During the Second World War hundreds
of thousands more Jews were transported into the
region, and executed by Axis forces. Today only
eight Jews remain in Kamenka.

A 'Wall of Heroes' marks the deeds of workers, soldiers and politicians near this central Tiraspol apartment complex. So many adults have moved abroad to find work that many school children live with their grandparents, or alone.

'You know, this is like a village school. The children are by nature accepting, patient. Few of them are rebellious.'

'And you?' I asked the teachers. 'Why haven't you moved away?'

'I've been trying for the last 20 years,' answered their soft-spoken colleague. 'I'm still trying.'

Beyond the school's dirt playground, the fields that once belonged to the collective farm lay fallow, and neat ranks of beech trees marched alongside the Dniester, tilting toward both the water and the setting sun.

'Pioneers, workers and school children! Struggle for the deepening of the lessening of international tension, for its expansion to all continents! Expose the efforts of the forces of aggression, revanchism and reaction – enemies of peace and the people's defence!'

15

Swan Song

'Where is my home?' the 'fixer' Marina Kereeva asked us over her second glass of champagne. 'My father was from the Urals. My mother from Moldova. My husband was part-Tartar. So what is my country? And what nationality are my children?'

Outside Tiraspol's Café Vienna, the winter wind whipped up the snow, driving it under the door, reminding me again of the maxim on the enduring beauty of Russian women. Inside the café two slices of ersatz-Sachertorte had put Marina in a buoyant mood. On our last evening together she was doubly determined to portray herself as carefree. Beside her on the banquette, New Soviet Man was arranging our next get-together, with his arm around her waist. 'We could have dinner together in London,' he suggested. 'Or Italy and make a weekend of it. Do you know the Osteria Francescana in Modena? Its *tagliatelle al ragù* is sublime.'

As he spoke, Marina raised her glass in a toast to him, and all men.

'Let those who never had me, let them be sad; and those who never wanted me, let them die.'

We had spent the day with five of Marina's favourite males, and

Tiraspol's Dixieland Liberty band is one of Transnistria's four state-sponsored musical acts. Jazz – with its strong connotations of freedom – was banned under Communism but Dixieland was permitted as 'the music of the American proletariat'.

Christ. In the glass-and-concrete Palace of Culture we'd dropped in on a rehearsal of one of the republic's official musical groups, the Dixieland Liberty band. Its charismatic founder Dimitri Sheremet had put down his banjo and leapt up to welcome us.

'I've always loved the Dixie sound,' enthused Sheremet. 'I feel as if I've known it since the day I was born.'

'It's music that makes me want to dance,' laughed his gangly, trumpeter Sasha Olhovich.

In the old Soviet Union everything that smacked of Western capitalism had been banned: Coca-Cola, Superman, free enterprise and jazz. But while jazz was considered capitalist, and its performance forbidden, New Orleans Dixieland was perceived as the music of the American proletariat. At school Sheremet and Olhovich had studied both classical and modern music, and on graduation Sheremet joined the Transnistria Symphony Orchestra.

'Which instrument do you prefer: French horn or banjo?' teased Olhovich.

'I have so much energy,' Sheremet replied with a laugh. 'I want to show my talent to everyone.'

Their band – dressed in matching grey pinstripe shirts and black Homburg hats – resumed the rehearsal, warming their instruments, chasing the cold out of the hall. Sheremet dropped his head forward as he plucked the banjo. Olhovich lifted his trumpet to his lips, muffled its mouth with his hat, stamped out the rhythm like a soldier marking time. The trombone wailed, the tuba puffed and five pairs of polished, pointed shoes tapped on the linoleum.

Beneath the crest of the republic swelled joyful, Dixieland versions of Ukrainian folk music and Russian pop songs. The recognition as state performers had brought Liberty an income and travel funds as well as the obligation to attend official functions.

'I hope we'll not be told what music to play,' said Sheremet with a nervous laugh.

Moldovan dancers perform a traditional dance in Tashlyk. In respect for the dominant culture, their act is sandwiched between performances of the 'Chunga Changa' and Michael Jackson's 'Thriller' – sung in Russian.

But when my host – again in sentimental frame of mind – asked for a Dixie rendition of the Soviet national anthem, Sheremet gravely shook his head.

'You above all should know that disrespectful American tradition hasn't reached us yet,' he said, suddenly serious, wary of satire. 'But we can play the Transnistrian anthem, without the banjo of course.'

No one pointed out that the two tunes are all but identical.

After the rehearsal we left the Palace of Culture and battled against the bitter winds to the city beach. In Transnistria – as elsewhere in the Orthodox world – the Epiphany brings the Great Blessing of Waters, when clergy and people process behind the Cross to the nearest body of water. On that day the Dniester was said to be imbued with special powers, and believers dipped themselves three times in the water, honouring the Holy Trinity, commemorating the baptism of Jesus and washing away the sins of the past year.

In winters when the Dniester froze over, the faithful cut holes in the ice, often in the shape of the cross. Luckily for Sheremet the river was only rimmed with ice this year. Along with 1,000 fellow believers, aged from six to 60, he stripped down to his underwear and plunged into the freezing waters, crossing himself, ducking his head again and again, readying himself for a spiritual rebirth. Marina stood beside me on the bank, holding his thermos of sweet Crimean mountain tea, enjoying the view.

'I feel such warmth in my heart,' Sheremet called out as icicles formed in his hair. 'Liberty forever,' he added in a kind of Slavic madness, and I didn't ask whether he was talking about his faith, his band or the country.

On that last evening at the Café Vienna it was wine rather than religion which warmed Marina's heart, plus the attention of New Soviet Man. As he flirted with her – and me – I wondered aloud about the hope for democracy in Transnistria, in its neighbour Ukraine and even in Russia itself. I reminded them of the satirists'

previous pages: A teenage ballroom dancer chats with friends before going on stage at the Soviet-era Palace of Culture in Tashlyk, a village half an hour's drive north of Tiraspol.

joke that Putin – and to a lesser extent the executives of Sheriff and my own super-elite host – aspired to rule like Stalin but live like Abramovich.

'We love the experience of democracy' – enthused New Soviet Man – 'when we are on holiday on the Côte d'Azur. That's why we don't need to have much of it at home.'

'But what about the common man?' I asked as a second bottle of champagne arrived at our table. Some 99.9% of citizens of the former Soviet Union hadn't had the chance to join the jet-setting international super-class. 'What about the dream of a society of equals?'

'As I told you before, freedom for the pike means death for the minnows,' New Soviet Man answered me.

'My country my country my country,' Marina interrupted, raising her glass again in a toast. She turned to me and said, 'I will tell you a story. Once far upstream on the Dniester there lived a boy with his mother. Their little farm was in a borderland, at the place where the frontiers of Moldova, Transnistria, Ukraine and Romania, even of Great Russia and Europe met.'

She sipped her wine and went on, 'One morning at the end of the Second World War the son left home to work in the family field across the river. In the evening when he rowed back he found barbed wire and Soviet soldiers on the beach. The guards told him that the river was now a border. They wouldn't let him come ashore, wouldn't let him go home, and he had to find a place to live on the far bank. Every day he toiled in the field, calling across the water to his mother, until the soldiers ordered him to stop. The old woman then started to sing songs to him, sharing the news from home: who had married, who had had a baby, who had died.

'In time the boy grew into a man, stopped farming the land and married. He trained to be a train driver, with a single, secret objective in mind.' Marina reached across the table, taking both our hands in

137

hers. 'Twenty-eight years after the border had torn his world apart, he drove a train across the river, stopped at his old village station, and finally, at last, embraced his mother again.'

'Is it true?' I – now a doubtful traveller – asked, looking from her to New Soviet Man and back again. We were thinking of the Transnistrian Supreme Court's audacious appeal for Russia to annex it, along with a large chunk of southern Ukraine for 'access'.

For a moment neither of them said a word.

'It is a story,' she replied, covering her mouth with her chocolate brown talons and laughing, laughing at the bittersweet tragedy.

Comrades, I ask you what is Transnistria? A utopia where men and women, united in their common historical choice, are forging a selfless post-Soviet identity? Or a Trojan Horse within which 'children of the sun' conjure up new illusions while practising yoga? Or perhaps the enclave is simply a profitable contrivance, slyly constructed by ambitious go-getters, where common people are all but irrelevant, apart from in giving legitimacy to the elite? All I know for sure is that Transnistria – the only place never to accept the collapse of the USSR – is part of a world where there are no more certainties.

At the end of the evening and at the bottom of too many bottles, we finished reliving the story of our journey, of heroic adventures and dubious deeds, of golden handshakes and sweetheart deals, of strategic tweets and Bentley SUVs, of 'fairness', fear and the hope of a better future.

'I wonder if you are looking for something which never existed?' my host finally asked me as we stood to leave, speaking with a new candidness. 'I am *Homo Sovieticus* like Marina,' he said, using for the first time the cynical, pseudo-Latin corruption of New Soviet Man. 'We grew up under the same system. So we know the illusions. And we know reality. Above all we know our people and how to treat them. And I tell you that the only way to get them to act or to change

140

previous pages: At the Epiphany as many as one thousand Transnistrians plunge into the frozen Dniester, dipping themselves three times to honour the Holy Trinity, to wash away their sins from the past year, and to experience a sense of spiritual rebirth. No figures exist for subsequent cases of pneumonia.

their ways is to point a gun at their heads, and threaten to shoot.'

'And if they still don't change?' I replied, too shocked by his candour to know how else to respond.

'Then one pulls the trigger.'

With that, and a final wink, my elusive, exclusive host slipped away into the night and his Bentley, vanishing back into his hidden, moneyed world as if we had never met.

.

overleaf: Russia refuses to withdraw its 2,000
'peace-keeping' troops from Transnistria, creating
a hurdle to Moldova's potential NATO membership.
As Moscow undermines that country's fragile
democracy, some commentators predict Moldova
will become 'the next Ukraine'. Others believe that
the Dniester between Moldova and Transnistria
is destined to become the new Berlin Wall.

Transnistrian timeline

56AD Romans occupy southern Transnistrian province of Lower Moesia, only to be elbowed out by barbarians, who are dislodged by Slavic tribes, who are sent packing by Turkic nomads, establishing a tradition which endures for two millennia.

1241 Transnistria occupied by Mongols.

1500 Transnistria snatched by the Grand Duchy of Lithuania.

1569 Transnistria seized by the Polish–Lithuanian Commonwealth.

1792 Transnistria absorbed into the Russian Empire.

1800s Transnistria, now designated as part of 'Bessarabia', is sometimes Russian, sometimes Moldovan, sometimes Romanian.

1940 Soviet occupation of Bessarabia and Northern Bukovina leads to the creation of the Moldavian SSR.

1941 Nazi and Romanian troops take over Transnistria. Jews and Communists deported to death camps.

1944 Red Army takes it back. Moldovans and Fascists deported to gulags.

1989 Berlin Wall falls burying the old stereotypes under the rubble. Yet Moldova declares Moldovan to be the country's only official language, carrying on the tradition of cultural chauvinism, giving Transnistria the finger.

1990 Transnistria declares independence, asserting its right to speak Transnistrian (which is identical to Moldovan). As many as a thousand civilians are killed in the ensuing conflict.

1992 Moscow sends in its 'peace keepers' (i.e. the former Soviet 14th Guards Army). Russian General Alexander Lebed tells 'the hooligans in Tiraspol and the fascists in Chisinau, either you stop killing each other or I'll shoot the whole lot of you with my tanks'. War of Transnistria ends. Igor Smirnov becomes president.

1993 Viktor Gushan and Ilya Kazmaly, former members of the KGB, create Sheriff, the company which will come to dominate business in the unrecognised state.

1994 Soviet Army withdraws from East Germany, dropping off 40,000 tons of ammunition for safe-keeping in Transnistria. Much of it soon goes missing.

2005 Sheriff, now richer than the country, supports the formation of the political party Renewal, with the intention of deposing Smirnov.

2011 Smirnov loses election, and vanishes from public eye.

2012 Ninety per cent of Transnistria's gold reserves also go missing. New president Yevgeny Shevchuk finds only $49,000 in state piggybank. Sheriff offers to extend credit.

2014 Inspired by the Crimea's example, the Transnistrian Supreme Court appeals for Moscow to draft a law that will allow the breakaway region to join Russia.

2015 On discovery of 67 Moldovan parliamentarians holidaying on New Soviet Man's mega-*yachtski* off Monte Carlo, EU suspends further integration of the Republic of Moldova. Transnistria joins its Eurasian Union.

2016 FC Sheriff buys Lionel Messi from Barcelona for $60,000,000.

2017 Yevgeny Shevchuk, president of newly united Moldov–Dnestria, takes seat at United Nations. Prime Minister Nina Shtanski gives birth to triplets.

2020 Moldov–Dnestria wins the Eurovision Song Contest.

2022 Vladimir Putin retires to Kamenka and takes up gardening. Italy – as holder of the revolving presidency of the new German-free Eurozone – relocates Europe's *de facto* capital from Brussels to Tiraspol, thereby returning to Lower Moesia after 2,000 years' absence.

2023 Tatiana Kushmir's shoe tree sprouts Prada sandals.

A note about the typeface

This book is set in Haultin, a typeface designed by the Dutch graphic and type designer Fred Smeijers (b. 1961) and inspired by the work of Pierre Haultin.

Though a contemporary of Claude Garamont and Robert Granjon, respective creators of the popular Garamond and Civilité typefaces, Pierre Haultin (c. 1510–86) – prolific in his output throughout that time – is less widely known as a type designer of the sixteenth century.

A Protestant, Haultin fled from France to Geneva as part of an exodus responding to the increasingly repressive religious legislation put in place by King Henry II and French Parliament from 1548 onwards. He was not the only craftsman to flee to Geneva, which became a formidable melting pot of creativity, especially print-related (there were three printers firms in Geneva in the 1540s; by the mid-fifties 22 were operating).

Haultin was a key player in the printing and publishing campaign that brought pocket-sized devotional and scriptural books to the French-speaking world, designing specifically for this purpose a compact but readable type at the extreme end of the height spectrum (6 points high by modern standards). Puzzlingly, he is also recorded in the same period as being indicted or jailed four times – once every year for a period of four years – for scoffing at the Scripture and for '*paillardise*' (lechery).

Acknowledgments

Many generous souls helped to make this book possible, first and foremost the people of Transnistria who welcomed us into their homes, offices, pig sheds and two-tiered Luxema swim spa Jacuzzi (with minibar, flat-screen TV and inbuilt sound system). We would like to thank them as well as Captain Paul-Henri Arni who first told us of the free-roaming anacondas at the Ministry of Justice. Huge thanks is also due to the Winston Churchill Memorial Trust for the Travel Fellowship that enabled us to make our journey beyond the Dniester, and to Jamie Balfour, Julia Weston and Alex Sibun for their support. Toby Latta, Ulrich Büchsenschütz, Dr Oliver Scholz and Elena Sukharkova of Control Risks provided invaluable insights into the republic, as did the former British Ambassador to Moldova Keith Shannon and IOM in Chisinau. For their guidance into the Russian mind (and timely translations) we are grateful to Alexandr Cliuicov, Melissa Eddy and others who wish to remain unnamed (those dual taxation agreements can be so tiresome). Finally, we may have missed the first Russian Revolution but we have joined a revolution in publishing. At Unbound, the heroic people's crowd-source publisher, we thank Justin Pollard, John Mitchinson and Jimmy Leach as well as Isobel Frankish and Cathy Hurren. Above all of course, our heartfelt thanks goes to our hundreds of supporters as well as our extended families.

Subscribers

Unbound is a new kind of publishing house.
Our books are funded directly by readers. This
was a very popular idea during the late eighteenth
and early nineteenth centuries. Now we have
revived it for the internet age. It allows authors
to write the books they really want to write and
readers to support the writing they would most
like to see published.

The names listed in this section are of readers
who have pledged their support and made this
book happen. If you'd like to join them, visit:
www.unbound.co.uk.

Andres Aguayo
Anand Aithal
Ali Akay
Oguz Akay
Moustafa Al Yassin
Sam Alexandroni
Hugh Andrew
Prune Antoine
Paul-Henri Arni
Fiona Arrigo
Chris Ash
Nesher G. Asner
Aurore
Mark Azavedo
Alex Baird
Sally Baker
Jamie Balfour
Kirsty Baring
Amy Jane Barnes
Andrea Barsony
Verona Bass
Paul Basson
Jonathan Bates
David Bawden
Jack Belleperche
Jilly Bennett
Jeanne Marie Berck
Joseph Bergen
Mark Bergman
Mark Bitel
Owen Blacker
Barry Blackmore
Christof Bojanowski
Wesley Bonar
Martyn Bond
Sylvie Bouny
Gary Brame
Nicholas Brewer
Tom Broadbent
Corinna
  Brocher-Behm
M Brown
Veronica
  Bruce-Gardner
Jennifer Brush

Alexis Bulgari
Jan Bullerdieck
Isabel Burford
Sarah Burrell
Louise Byrne
Werner Cabooter
Alberto Cairo
Angela Caldwell
Laurie Campbell
Judy Carlton
Nicolas Carrillo
Barry Caruth
Nancy Chapple
Mary Chard
Charles
Marilyn Charlton
Mark Charlton
Michael Charlton
Elisa Chiu
Chris Christian
Peter Clark
Clive Cockram
Simon Coley
Jo Cope
Laurent Corbaz
John Crawford
Susan Crean
Lizanne Crowther
Bailey Curtis
Daniel Danziger
Richard Danziger
Stuart Davidson
Ceri Davies
Gwen Davies
Nick Davies
Sara Davies
Louise de Lima
Jenny Dearden
Bérénice Debras
Roland Degois
Anne Delforge
Marie-Luce Delforge
Scott Donaldson
Lyse Doucet
Christian Drury

Jane Dubuisson
Celina Dunlop
Caroline Eckersley
Melissa Eddy
Victoria Edwards
Chris Elliott
Tomas Eriksson
Eugenie
Peter Evans
Robyn Eyde
Claude Fabbretti
Charles Fairey
Jumoke Fashola
Sam Faulkner
Josey Ferrer
RoseMarie
  FitzSimons
David Foreman
Yvonne Forward
Ilana Fox
Caroline
  Frances-King
Isobel Frankish
Jens Füting
Mark Gamble
Diana Garnham
John Garrett
Jorge Garzon
Jennifer Gascoigne
John Gaye
Niki George
Vania George
William George
Susan Gibson
Mary Ginsberg
Claire Glasscoe
Will Goble
Colin Godfrey MBE
Andrea Goldman
Nikolai Gorshkov
Terence Gould
Jacky Gourlaouen
Scott Griffin
Mike Griffiths
Anne Marie Grobet

Vincent Guiry
Miranda Hadfield
Gary Haigh
Patrycja Haines
Linnane Haley
Tarquin Hall
Julia Hammond
  Johnson
Janie Hampton
Michael F. Hancock
Barry Hankey
Di Harris
Caitlin Harvey
Mike Harwood
Andrew Hearse
Bea Hemming
Gerald Hewitson
Christopher Hird
Dean Hodge
Samantha
  Holdsworth
John A. Holland
Ann Horne
Sally J. Howard
Andy Howell
Kathrin Hoyos
Mark Hudson
Matt Huggins
Paul Hyland
Bill Jeffries
Paul Jeorrett
Arild Sæther
  Johannessen
Marjorie Johns
Chris Johnson
David Johnson
Richard Johnson
Cambridge Jones
Dafydd Jones
Rosy Jones
Siddhi Joshi
Terry Kane
Michael Keating
Richard Keatinge
Andrew Kelly

Tom Kennedy
Marian
 Kermanshahchi
James Kerr
Alex Kerridge
Rik Kershaw-Moore
Siri Trang Khalsa
Dan Kieran
Lucian Kim
Tom Kinter
Dan Klein
Maureen Korp, PhD
Eddie Korvin
Comrade Mark
 Kozakiewicz
Alexander Krueger
My-Linh Kunst
Robert Lacey
Domitille Lagourgue
Daniel Lak
Doug Latta
Toby Latta
Simon Lawrence
Linden Lawson
Tim Lawson
Lelei LeLaulu
Piers Le Marchant
Silvia Le Marchant
Jimmy Leach
Ian Ledger
Orla Lehane
Beth Lewis
Edward Lewis
Sarah Lewis
Philip Lines
Robert Lisak
Peter and
 Deborah Lloyd
Sara Lovett
John Low
James Lupolt
Kristina Lutz
Chris MacAllister
Catriona Macaulay
John McCarthy

Kate McCormack
Kevin McCullough
Angus Macdonald
Ian MacDonald
Susan McDonald
Robert Macfarlane
Stryker McGuire
John Mackedon
Ina Mclaughlin
Andrew MacLean
Patrick McLean
Michael MacMillan
Fenella McVey
Manchán Magan
John Maher
Christopher
 Manchigiah
Jessica Mander
Roberta Margison
Neil Matthews
Eva Menuhin
Denise Meredith
Ian Millar
Jan Miller-Klein
Claudia Modonesi
Michelle Molloy
Jean-Michel Monod
Rachel & Neil Moss
G C Mosse
Andrew Mueller
Karen Neale
Graham Nelson
Jane Nicholls
Jinx Nolan
Mark O'Neill
Francis Oglethorpe
Barry Kevin Oliphant
Aaron Ostrovsky
Murat Ozkasim
Jack Page
Michael Paley
Bernard Pasquier
Joost Perreijn
Ryszard Piotrowicz
Robert Pledge

Justin Pollard
Steve Porte
John Porter
Adam Priestley
Jacqueline Pritchard
Jon Prosser
Eugenie Radziwill
Andrew Rasbash
Walter Raymond
Eliza Reid
Dinah Reynolds
Robin Richards
Eric Roberts
Hilary Roberts
Keith Roberts
Lee Roberts
Miles Robinson
Stuart Robinson
Petre Rodan
Sam Rose
Lucille Rosenqvist
Dana Samson
Christoph Sander
Katja Sass
Tiziana Savinelli
Francis Scarr
Christian Scheja
S. Schmidt
Klaus Joachim
 Schmitz
Helena Scott
Penny Scott-Bayfield
Rosemary Scoular
Ruth Segal
Kathleen Seidel
Keith Shannon
Tamsin and Mark
 Shelton
Neville Shulman CBE
Alexandra Sibun
Alan Sinclair
Mark Slater
Nick Smith
Piers Smith-Cresswell
Doug Snyder

Nicholas Snyder
David Somers
Sarah Spankie
Frank Stella
David Stelling
Richard &
 Fiona Stewart
Michael Storey
Michael Strawson
Jérémy Taburchi
Peter Tait
Kenny Taylor
Veronique
 Thierry-Scully
Matthew Tinker
Christopher Trent
David G Tubby
Nick Tucker
Edmund Tustian
Thomas Underwood
Andreas Uthoff
Wieland Van Dijk
Gail von Bergen-Ryan
Juliette von Seibold
Michael Walsh
Jia Wang
Amy Wares
Gerald Watson
Jorgen Westad
Julia Weston
Florian Westphal
Richard Wheeler
Ben Whitehouse
Andrew Wiggins
Brian Williams
Dick Willis
Lynette Willoughby
Guy Wilmot
Wendy Wilmot
Johanna Wilson
Elizabeth Winter
Steve Woodward
Ed Wright
Katherine York
Nicola Young

overleaf: 'Long live our great Motherland –
the Union of Soviet Socialist Republics!'